Gifts for Herb Lovers

Over 50 Projects to Make and Give

BETTY OPPENHEIMER

A Storey Publishing Book

STOREY

STOREY COMMUNICATIONS, INC.
SCHOOLHOUSE ROAD
POWNAL, VERMONT 05261

*The mission of Storey Communications is to serve our customers
by publishing practical information that encourages personal
independence in harmony with the environment.*

Edited by Deborah Balmuth and Bonnie Dyer-Bennet
Designed by Meredith Maker
Text production by Eugenie S. Delaney
Production assistance by Erin Lincourt and Leslie Noyes
Cover and finished project illustration by Frank Riccio
Line drawings by Brigita Fuhrmann
Indexed by Northwind Editorial Services

Projects on the following pages are excerpted or adapted from previously published Storey books:

page 11 from *Herb Mixtures and Spicy Blends;* page 16 from *Herbal Vinegar;* pages 22 & 29 from *The Herbal Body Book;*
pages 24 & 66 from *Herbal Treasures;* page 27 from *The Essential Oils Book;* page 46 from *Nature Printing;*
and page 48 from *Making Your Own Paper.*

Storey Publishing books are available for special premium and
promotional uses and for customized editions. For further
information, please call the Custom Publishing Department
at 1-800-793-9396.

Printed in the United States by R. R. Donnelley
10 9 8 7 6 5 4 3 2 1

Library of Congress Cataloging-in-Publication Data

Oppenheimer, Betty, 1957-
    Gifts for herb lovers: over 50 projects to make and give /
Betty Oppenheimer.
        p.   cm.
    Includes bibliographical references and index.
    "A Storey Publishing Book"
    ISBN 0-88266-983-4 (pbk. : alk. paper)
    1. Nature craft. 2. Herbs—Utilization. I. Title.
TT157.067   1997
745.5—dc21   97-13882
                                                              CIP

CONTENTS

CHAPTER 7: *Techniques*

To my husband Irv, whose love is as warm and
healing as an herbal tea, whose support is as strong
as an ancient Douglas Fir tree, and whose faith
guides me like the light of the Harvest Moon.

INTRODUCTION

This book is about gifts — the gifts nature has bestowed upon us in the form of herbs, the gifts we give ourselves when we take time to learn about and cultivate herbs, and the hand-crafted gifts we can offer to our friends and loved ones, using herbs as raw materials. Herbs, flowers, leaves, spices, and seeds — all are included in these pages for their scents, flavors, and decorative shapes and colors.

Nature offers us a great gift in plants. Working with plant materials can be a lifelong educational experience, and offers a way to use what is around us in creative ways. Gardening and crafting are relaxing and rewarding in themselves, and the joys of giving and receiving hand-crafted gifts cannot be equaled by anything found in a store.

Whether or not you garden, you can enjoy the pleasures of herbs in your food, your bath, or decorating your home. The projects in this book offer ways to use herbs as raw materials in culinary, cosmetic, scented, and decorative products. Herb motifs can be used in painting, stamping, stenciling, printing, stitching, and sculpting. It is my hope that the techniques and suggestions I offer will stimulate your creative spirit to experiment and develop your personal favorites. Please don't

limit yourself to the specific projects I have outlined — mix and match the various techniques to make the creations of your imagination and the objects you find of practical use.

Transforming a simple herb into a wonderful gift is half the fun of these crafts! The wrapping and greetings you offer can be as much a part of its enjoyment as the gift itself. Share the history, lore, and knowledge of herbs along with the herbal gifts to make them doubly special; you just may spark a friend's interest in exploring further.

Long ago, the knowledge of herbal remedies was, indeed, a gift. Those who knew how to concoct teas, ointments, poultices, and other remedies were valued for their healing powers. In the 16th century (more than 4000 years after the Chinese began studying and documenting the medicinal value of herbs), the Great Age of Herbals took place in Europe. Many comprehensive books were written on the subject of herbs and their uses, allowing others to learn the art and science of herbs. (Some of these books are available today.) The early herbalists were the predecessors of modern botanists and physicians, and their recipes were well-guarded secrets. Now, however, their mysterious concoctions are ours for the asking,

to the extent that we are willing to learn and experiment. For us — the late-20th-century herbalists — an amazing variety of plant material and information is available.

Nature offers us endless possibilities! You don't need a traditional herb garden to carry out these projects. Pick up pinecones in the forest, wildflowers along the roadside, spices from your local grocery or your favorite herb catalog, and preserve them to create wonderful gifts. Creating with herbs, seeds, flowers, and spices is a lifelong learning process, and will inspire you to collect and identify interesting plants, experiment with blends of flavor, scent, and color, and share these gifts with friends.

Take advantage of the gifts of nature, knowledge, technology, and particularly, the gift of time. We have so much more time for creative exploration than did our ancestors, who needed most of their energy simply to survive. Learn, and share, and play in the realm of nature's bounty. The gifts you give will return to you tenfold, in the joyous sensory pleasures derived from the fruits of your labors.

Verily great grace may go
With a little gift; and precious are all things
that come from friends.
— Theocritus (310–250 B.C.), *Idylls*

2

CHAPTER 1

Culinary and Preserving Gifts

These gifts offer a variety of practical and decorative ways to preserve and use herbs. Each of the eight projects makes a wonderful gift, but also serves as a jumping-off point for further use of the herbs in cooking or crafts. The first two projects — basic tools for drying and pressing herbs, leaves, and flowers — are made of wood. The remaining projects in this chapter use mixes of plant materials to stimulate the senses of taste and smell.

Herb Drying Rack

This pegged, wooden wall rack would be a practical and welcome gift for anyone who dries fresh plant material during the harvest season for use in cooking and craft projects throughout the year. You can decorate the rack in as simple or as ornate a manner as you choose. (See pages 109–115 for options.)

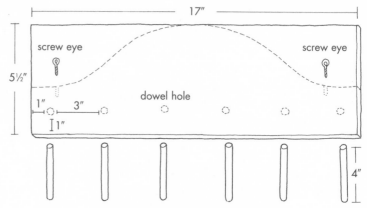

MATERIALS

One 5½″ x 17″ piece of ¾″ pine
   (called a 1 x 6 at the lumberyard)
½″-diameter wooden dowel, 24″ long
Sandpaper, medium- and fine-grit
   sheets
Water-based primer
Water-based paint (colors of your
   choice)
Carpenter's wood glue
2 small screw eyes
Clear wood finish (optional)

EQUIPMENT

Ruler or yardstick
Hand coping saw or electric jigsaw
½″ drill bit and electric drill
Brushes, for stenciling (optional)
Stencils (optional)
Small brush for gluing

1 With a pencil, mark the center point along the 17″ length of the pine. Outline and then saw the curved shape for the top of the herb rack.

2 Saw the dowel into six 4″ lengths.

3 Measure 1″ up from the bottom of the wood panel and draw a light pencil line. Mark 1″ in from each edge and every 3″ across this line for the peg holes. Drill the ½″ holes where the pencil lines cross, at each mark. Be careful to drill a straight hole.

17″

screw eye   screw eye

5½″

dowel hole

1″   3″

1″

4″

Cutting and assembling diagram

4

4 Starting with the medium-grit sandpaper and continuing with the fine-grit sandpaper, sand the edges of the panel, the protruding end of the dowels, and the exterior of the drilled holes.

5 If you plan to paint the entire surface of the wood, coat it first with primer. If you would prefer to leave wood exposed and to paint a design only, brush on a "blotch" — a primed background underneath the design area only. This will coat the wood and prevent the paint from being absorbed into the wood grain. When the primer is dry, decorate the panel by stenciling, stamping, printing, or painting. Paint the dowels to match your design, but leave unpainted ¾″ at one end of each peg, for better glue adhesion.

6 When all of the paint has dried, brush wood glue into the peg holes and onto the unpainted dowel ends. Push a dowel into each hole and wipe off excess glue. Allow glue to dry thoroughly.

7 To attach screw eyes for hanging, mark two points along the top of the rack, 1″ from each side edge and ¼″ from the back edge. Screw in the eyes at these points.

8 Touch up any paint that may have been disturbed when you glued the peg or attached the screw eye. Brush wood finish onto the entire piece, front and back, for a professional look.

Suggested Use ❧

Tie leafy green herbs and firm flowers in bunches, using twine or wire, and hang them upside down from each peg until dry. (Dry in a cool, dark place with good ventilation.)

As soon as the plants are thoroughly dry, strip the leaves off the stems and store in airtight containers to preserve their flavor and aroma.

This drying rack is perfect for kitchen classics such as sage, rosemary, thyme, marjoram, and oregano, and also works for drying various seedpods and flower buds.

Leaf and Flower Press

This press offers endless possibilities for preserving beautiful flowers for decorative use, and provides the flattened material used in nature printing. (See pages 113 – 115 for techniques.)

MATERIALS

½" plywood (or two 7" x 7" square
   store-bought wood plaques)
Sandpaper, medium- and fine-grit
Paints for decorating (optional)
Varnish or wood wax (optional)
Smooth cardboard
Absorbent paper (paper towels or
   unprinted newsprint)
Four 5" bolts, with 4 wing nuts and
   8 flat washers

EQUIPMENT

Pencil
Ruler or yardstick
Hand saw
Clamp
Drill and drill bit larger than
   diameter of bolts
Mat, X-acto, or box knife
Metal ruler

1 Cut the plywood into two 7" squares. If you like, you may round the corners by using a coping saw and sanding the edges smooth.

2 Measure and draw a line ¾" from each edge on the top wood square. Clamp the two pieces together. At the point of intersection at each corner, drill through both pieces of wood.

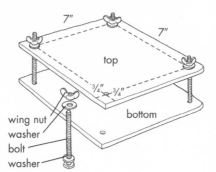

3 Smooth the edges of the wood and the surfaces disturbed by the drilling, first with medium-grit sandpaper, then with fine-grit sandpaper.

4 If you plan to decorate the press, remember that the "top" is the side with the wing nuts. You can paint, stencil, stamp, or print on the wood, or simply finish the wood with wax or varnish.

5 Cut the cardboard into 7" squares. You will need two pieces for each layer of plant material. Your press will hold about 20 layers. The edges must be mitered to fit inside the bolts. Measure and mark center point along each side edge of

the squares. Mark each side, out 2½" in either direction from these points. Connect the corners to create triangles.

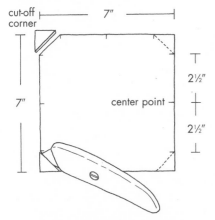

cut-off corner

7"

7"

center point

2½"

2½"

Cut the triangles off with a mat or X-acto knife, cutting against a metal ruler. The absorbent paper must be cut in the same shape. Use a cut piece of cardboard as a pattern, trace onto several layers of paper towel, and cut with knife or scissors.

6 To assemble the press, layer cardboard, one sheet of paper, the plant material, one sheet of paper, then cardboard again. Continue with layers of cardboard, paper, and plant until your press is full, but not higher than the 5" bolts. Place a washer onto each bolt and thread each

bolt through its hole in the two pieces of plywood. Then place another washer and a wing nut on each bolt and tighten the press, applying even pressure among the four corners.

To Use

Collect leaves and flowers that lend themselves to pressing (see sidebar). If you will not be pressing the specimens immediately, put them in zip-seal bags filled with air and store in a cool place (preferably the refrigerator). When you're ready to press, use a soft brush to remove any debris from the plant material, and place it on the towel or newsprint. Fit as many items as you can on each layer, without allowing them to touch each other. Pile up the cardboard, towel, and plant layers; put the plywood on top; and tighten the press. Change the paper towel or newsprint daily; depending on the plant material, it will take 1–2 weeks for them to dry thoroughly. *Note:* If you are pressing leaves and flowers for nature printing, it may not be necessary to dry them completely, but, rather, just enough to flatten them for inking. (See pages 113–115 for techniques.)

Plants for Pressing ↬

Almost any leaf can be pressed, but when it comes to flowers, start with relatively flat ones, like pansies and cosmos, or dry single petals. When you're confident enough to try bulkier flowers, choose ones with small calyxes, or remove some of the bulk from the back of the flower, allowing the front to appear flatter.

It is also possible to "pad" certain areas of the flower, within the press, so that the padding presses on the flat areas while the press flattens onto the high points. To do this, fold pads of paper equal in thickness to the high points, or thickest parts, of the flower or stem, and shaped to fit around the thick part while pressing on the thin areas.

Bouquet Garni Wreath

A culinary herb wreath in the kitchen offers stimulation for the senses! It looks great, smells wonderful, and provides freshly dried herbs for all of your culinary creations. Fresh herbs tucked into a raffia braid will dry in place, and they can be replenished, so your wreath will last for years as a kitchen staple.

MATERIALS

Thick hank of raffia, about 2″ in diameter, plus several spare strands

Yarn needle

One 9″ wire wreath frame

Fresh sage, thyme, oregano, tarragon, or other culinary herbs

Dried chili peppers, for color (optional)

1 Tie one end of the raffia hank firmly with a spare length of raffia.

2 Divide the hank into three sections. Braid it, working it into a curve to match the wire wreath.

3 Tie off the other end.

4 Working with the frame side up, sew the braid to the frame, using the needle threaded with the spare length of raffia. Keep the stitches hidden on the back of the wreath, and bend the braid so that it lies flat.

5 When the frame is completely covered, lay the end of the braid over the start and bind tightly with raffia, giving the illusion of a bow. Trim the ends so that they are even.

6 Tie the herbs into small bundles and tuck them into the braid, distributing them evenly around the wreath. The bundles can be of single herbs or a combination of bouquet garni herbs, which can then be used to season a classic dish.

7 For hanging the wreath, make a raffia loop and connect it to the braid and/or wire frame at the top.

8 If you are giving the wreath to someone who is unfamiliar with whole-leaf herbs, make a card or label that identifies what is in the wreath, and what each herb looks like.

Straw wreath

Using a premade straw wreath, attach the herb bundles directly into the straw, or loosely wire them around the wreath using green florist wire. If you arrange the bundles so that they are all inserted with the leaves facing upward, you will always be able to pull up to remove a bundle of herbs and push down to insert a new one.

Styrofoam wreath

Styrofoam rings can be used (they come in green or white), either by pushing the stems of the herbs directly into the foam or by using floral picks. (Floral picks are wooden picks with an attached wire used to attach the plant material and hold it slightly away from the foam surface.)

When using the herbs from this type of wreath, a pick may be removed, emptied, refilled with fresh herbs, and then pushed back into the foam.

Grapevine wreath

Using vine wreaths is a more decorative way to display the herbs, and you will probably want some of the vine to show as well, since it has lovely, organic curves. Decide where you want the herb bunches to go and wire them in loosely with florist wire so that they can be easily removed. If you are decorating with nonedible plant materials, use a hot glue gun to attach these items permanently.

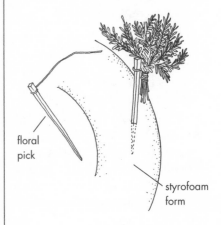

floral pick

styrofoam form

Bouquet Garni Bags

To make your wreath a more formal gift, include some cheesecloth bags with it, so that a traditional bouquet garni can be made with the herbs you have used. Purchase cheesecloth bags from a culinary herb supplier, or make your own using one of the methods below.

These bags are discarded after use, so there is no need to make a finished drawstring casing. If you practice recycling, though, and you want to make reusable bags, use Method 3.

Whichever way you decide to make the bags, leave the tie string long enough for it to be tied around the handle as it dangles in the stewpot, so that it can be easily removed without having to fish it out.

Method 1. Cut 6″ squares of cheesecloth, fill with herbs, and tie closed with cotton string or unwaxed dental floss.

Method 2. Sew two 2½″–4″ rectangles of cheesecloth together on three sides. To make the drawstring, thread a needle with the string or floss and weave it in and out of the unsewn edge, ½″ from the raw edge. Fill with herbs, cinch, and tie the drawstring closed.

Method 3. Make a bag using Method 2, but then turn under the raw edge twice and stitch a ¼″ casing (tunnel) for the string, leaving a small opening at the ends of the casing. Thread the string through the casing, using a safety pin to push it through, and tie the string ends together to create the drawstring loop.

Herbal Lore ∽

Traditionally, a bouquet garni is a bundle of herbs, wrapped in cheesecloth or a tea ball, used to season soups, stews, and sauces and removed before serving. The herbs flavor, but are not present in, the final dish. Bouquet garni herbs include parsley, thyme, bay leaf, basil, chervil, celery, tarragon, burnet, rosemary, and savory. If you are making your own mix, you can also add peppercorns and other whole spices such as allspice and cloves. The same method of bagging herbs and spices is used to make mulled cider or wine, but cinnamon, citrus peel, and cloves take the place of aromatic, leafy green herbs.

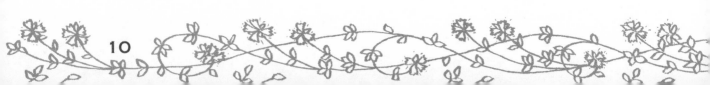

Culinary Herb Mixtures

These herb mixtures are but a tiny sampling of the many combinations you can create for the kitchen. Offered as gifts for friends with no time to cook, these blends are sure to be appreciated for their freshness, flavor, and ease of use. For hard-to-find herbs, see page 117.

Thyme and Seasons Curry Blend

Makes about ⅔ cup

- 4 tablespoons dried coriander
- 2 tablespoons ground turmeric
- 1½ tablespoons ground cumin
- 1 tablespoon ground fenugreek
- 1½ teaspoons ground black pepper
- 1½ teaspoons poppy seeds
- 1½ teaspoons ground dried red chilies
- ¾ teaspoon dried mustard
- ½ teaspoon ground cardamom

Blend ingredients in a mixing bowl. Store in an airtight jar away from heat. Use with meats, poultry, eggs, combined with peanut butter or coconut milk for a Thai flavor, or as a condiment on the side.

The Rosemary House's Seed Blend

Makes about 2 cups

- 6 tablespoons whole allspice berries
- 6 tablespoons black peppercorns
- 3 tablespoons green peppercorns
- 3 tablespoons whole mustard seed
- 3 tablespoons whole coriander seed
- 2 tablespoons whole fennel seed
- 2 tablespoons whole dill seed
- 2 tablespoons white peppercorns
- 1 tablespoon pine peppercorns (optional)
- 1 tablespoon dried chili peppers

Combine ingredients and store in an airtight container or a pepper mill. Grind as needed.

Use on vegetables, stews, and egg dishes.

No-Salt Mix

Makes about ¾ cup

- 6 tablespoons dried dulse seaweed
- 3 tablespoons kelp powder
- 3 tablespoons onion granules or flakes
- 1 tablespoon black peppercorns
- 1 tablespoon dried parsley
- 1 tablespoon dried lemon zest

Grind all ingredients together in a food processor. Store in an airtight container, or keep in a pepper mill for use at the table. Add other aromatic herbs as desired.

Herb and Garlic Braid

Individual cloves of garlic are planted in the fall, and by the end of the following summer, each has grown into a cluster (head) hidden beneath the soil, under long stems that lend themselves perfectly to braiding. A garlic braid can be embellished with whatever herbs and dried flowers you have available, or choose a combination to suit a friend's taste buds and decor.

MATERIALS

Freshly harvested garlic heads with
  stems left on
Fresh or dried herbs and flowers
Twine or ¼″ wide ribbon
Floral wire

1 Hang the garlic in a dry place for a day or two to dry the attached soil and enable you to brush it off the heads. If your garlic has flowered, you may want to incorporate these into the braid, but to do so, they must be cut off the top of the stem and woven in separately. Garlic flowers, which are large and spherical, dry nicely.

2 With the herbs and flowers you have chosen (you can add chili peppers, too) and using wire or twist ties, make small bunches of plant material. If you expect that this braid will be used for seasoning, keep each herb separate so that it is easily identifiable.

In some braids, the herbs hide the garlic stems; other braids have sprays of herbs scattered throughout. Depending on what you have in mind, you will need many or few bunches of herbs, but for the sake of this project, let's say 1 bunch of herbs for each 3 garlic heads.

3 Lay the first three garlic heads on your working surface, stems toward you, and begin the braid, overlapping the right-hand stem to the middle, then the left-hand stem to the middle. Now add a fourth garlic head above the first three, on the right side, and braid it, with the current right-hand stem, toward the center. You are braiding the back, and the garlic heads — now facing down on the table — will be the front. Take care to increase or decrease the tension on the braid to locate the heads exactly where you want them, leaving interesting spaces for your herb bundles later. The fifth head is

added in the center, the sixth on the left, and so on, always situating the garlic head toward the front of the garland and braiding the new stem along with the stem already in place, to interweave and hold each head where you want it to be.

4 When your braid is of the desired length, continue braiding the stems without adding more garlic. Fold the braid back around to form a large hanging loop, and wire the end of the braid securely back onto itself. Trim off any excess stem.

5 Turn over the braid — the garlic heads will then be facing you — and adjust their placement, if necessary. Tuck herb bunches into the braid, so that they silhouette the garlic heads in leaves and colors.

6 Using twine or ribbon, start at the bottom of the braid and anchor the bunches onto the braid. This can be done with bows or knots, or you can do it from the back, so that the twine does not show. If you really want the tying to be hidden, use wire instead of twine or ribbon.

7 Tie a long length of twine to the bottom of the braid, in the back. Anchor it with a knot every few inches up the back of the braid. Now begin wrapping around the braided loop, to reinforce it for hanging. This can be simple looping or braiding, or fancy macramé or crochet if you're handy with a needle. Finish off the twine ends by knotting securely in the back of the braid.

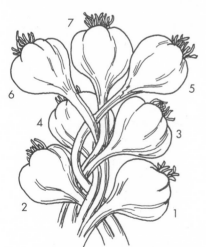

Tea Bags and Herbal Teas

Teas are a wonderful way to use herbs, flowers, seeds, and spices, and who doesn't enjoy relaxing with a cup? Herbal teas come in an assortment of flavors and aromas, and can be tailored to fit anyone's tastes. Package your custom blends in handmade bags for gift giving.

MATERIALS

Cheesecloth or muslin, cut into 4″ squares or circles

Cotton string or unwaxed dental floss

Oaktag or other card stock (index cards or file folders work well)

EQUIPMENT

Scissors

Hole punch or stapler

Needle and thread or sewing machine

1 Into the center of each piece of cloth, place 1 rounded tablespoon of tea.

2 Gather up the edges and wrap the string tightly around the bag several times.

3 Cut the card stock into small tags, about 1″ x 1″, and write on each tag the name of the tea, and ingredients. Punch a hole in one edge of each tag.

4 Pull one or both of the string ends through the hole in the tag, and tie a knot to secure it. (Instead of using a hole punch, you can staple the tag to the string.)

You can sew tea bags from cheesecloth, muslin, or lightweight sew-in (not fusible) interfacing. Starting with a 5″ x 30″ piece of fabric, fold it so that it measures 2½″ x 30″, and stitch the two layers together alternating 2″ and ½″ intervals.

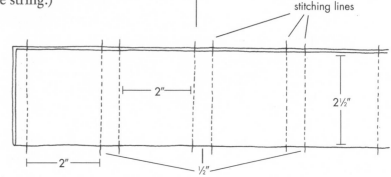

FINISHING THE BAGS

There are two different ways to finish the bags:

Method 1: Cut the bags apart between the ½″ stitch lines. Fill each with tea, then fold down the corners and then the top. Use a staple to close each bag, and attach a string with tag to each bag. These bags look more like a commercial tea bag than do the others.

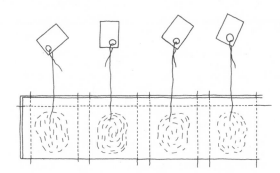

Method 2: While they are still connected, fill each bag with 1 tablespoon of tea. Stitch across the entire row of 12 bags, catching a length of string at the top of each pouch. Use the string to tie on a label tag.

Tea Blends ❧

All herbs should be dried. Start by blending equal parts of each ingredient; then adjust to your own taste. Each cup of blend mixture yields 12 to 14 tea bags.

Basic Two-Herb Tea
Option 1:
  Rosemary
  Lavender
Option 2:
  Dried citrus zest
  Anise seeds

Basic Three-Herb Tea
Hibiscus petals
Rose hips
Lemon verbena leaves

Ground Seed Blend
Fennel seeds
Anise seeds
Coriander seeds
Caraway seeds

Minty Herb Blend
Birch leaves
Peppermint
Savory
Bee balm

Classic Blend
Lavender flowers
Rosemary
Lemon balm
Spearmint
Cloves

Vanilla Berry Blend
Strawberry leaves
Blackberry leaves
Sweet woodruff

Herbal Vinegars

Elegant to display and use, herbal vinegars have become important in today's cuisine. You can make herbal vinegars with white or red wine, cider, balsamic or sherry vinegars; experimenting with various flavors will help you decide which herbs taste best with which vinegars. The recipes on these pages each make about 2 cups.

Herb Vinegar

¼   cup fresh basil
¼   cup fresh oregano
6   cloves garlic
1   teaspoon black peppercorns
2   cups red wine vinegar

Fruit Vinegar

¼   cup fresh thyme
2   cups white wine vinegar
1   cup fresh raspberries

Spice Vinegar

1   teaspoon black peppercorns
1   teaspoon whole cloves
1   hot red chili pepper
1   quarter-sized piece of fresh gingerroot
2   cups balsamic vinegar

1   **For herb vinegar:** Combine all ingredients in a quart jar.

For fruit vinegar: Bruise the fruit and then combine with thyme and vinegar in a quart jar.

For spice vinegar: Combine all ingredients in a nonreactive metal or enamel pan and heat on stove to 110°F. (Or use glass bowl and heat to same temperature in microwave.) Pour into quart jar.

2   Seal jar with a nonmetallic lid (or line metal lid with plastic wrap).

3   Store jar in a dark place to steep. Shake every few days for 1 week to 1 month. The longer you steep the herbs, the stronger your vinegar will be. If you feel that your vinegar is not flavorful enough, strain out the first, steeped batch of herbs and replace them with more of the same combination of herbs. This will increase the concentration of flavors.

For fruit vinegar, you can sweeten by adding 3 tablespoons honey or ¼ cup sugar to the finished vinegar (after it has steeped with the fruit and herbs) and simmer for 3 minutes just before pouring into the bottles (see next step).

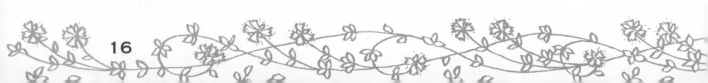

4 Sterilize vinegar bottles by washing in hot, soapy water with a bottle brush. Rinse well. Pour boiling water into each bottle, allow to sit for 10 minutes, pour out the water, and invert the bottles until ready to use. (Sterilize just before you are ready to use the bottles.)

5 Strain the vinegar and herb mixture through cheesecloth or a coffee filter placed in a strainer. Using a funnel, pour into sterilized bottles. For a festive touch, add a sprig of fresh herbs to the bottle.

6 Seal the bottle with a cork or with its original cap. For a decorative wax seal, see sidebar on this page.

7 On a self-adhesive label or a tag hung from a string around the bottle neck, indicate the type of vinegar and the date you made it. Vinegars are best used within 6 months, and should be stored in a dark place.

Corking a Bottle with a Waxed Ribbon Seal ❧

Push the cork well into the bottle. Melt enough paraffin in a double boiler (never melt wax directly over the heat source) to submerge the cork and the top 1″ of the glass bottle neck. You can use common household (jar-sealing) paraffin, available at your local grocery, or you can melt down candle ends. Color the paraffin by adding some grated crayons. Hold a piece of ribbon (4″–6″ long) over the cork so that it comes straight down the sides of the neck, and dip the bottle top into the wax. Remove from wax and allow to cool for 1 minute; then repeat the dipping process. If the coating of wax created by two dips is still very thin, your wax may be too hot. Remove the wax from the heat and allow it to cool for a few minutes before redipping. To unseal the wax, simply pull on the ribbon and uncork the bottle.

For a special gift, make a painted vinegar bottle (see page 40).

Spiced Pinecone Potpourri

This potpourri is wonderfully aromatic, reminiscent of an old-fashioned Christmas. The mixture is so visually appealing that it makes a beautiful display during the holidays. Some oils may be available at your local pharmacy. For hard-to-find ingredients, see page 117. For variations on potpourri, see page 108.

INGREDIENTS

Makes 2–4 cups (about 1 pound), depending on size of pinecones

6	ounces assorted pinecones (small to medium)
1½	drams (90 drops) of essential spice oils, as follows:
20	drops cinnamon oil
20	drops allspice oil
20	drops sweet orange or bergamot oil
15	drops clove oil
15	drops nutmeg oil
2	ounces dried orange peel (see sidebar), cut into strips or large pieces
1½	ounces orrisroot chunks or pieces
1	ounce cinnamon bark pieces
1	ounce whole hibiscus flowers
½	ounce bay leaves or lemon eucalyptus leaves

EQUIPMENT

Cookie sheet
Small paintbrush
Eyedropper
Quart jar with lid (larger if your pinecones are very big)

1 Heat the pinecones on the cookie sheet in a 150°F oven for 1 hour, to dry them and to kill any insects that may be living in them.

2 With a small brush, wipe any seeds, bugs, and debris off each cone.

3 Combine the oils and brush them onto the pinecones.

4 In a large jar, combine all ingredients. Replace lid and allow to set for 3 weeks, shaking often.

TO USE

This mixture makes a lovely splash of color in open bowls scattered throughout the house. A cellophane bag full, labeled and tied with ribbon, makes a nice preholiday gift to spruce up home or office. Store any unused potpourri in a sealed container so it will last as long as possible.

Drying Citrus Peel for Fragrant Potpourri

6 oranges with 2 tablespoons powdered orrisroot, or
6 lemons with 1½ tablespoons orrisroot, or
6 limes with 1 tablespoon powdered orrisroot

1 Thinly pare the outer rind from the fruit.

2 Rub the rinds with powdered orrisroot.

3 Place the peels on a nonstick baking sheet and place in a preheated 300°F oven for 2½ to 3 hours. Peels should be hard but not brittle.

4 Cool completely; then store in airtight containers.

5 Just before using, coarsely crush or bruise the peels with a mortar and pestle.

Dried Apples for Fragrant Potpourri, Wreaths, and Garlands

2 pounds apples
¼ cup lemon juice
1 teaspoon salt

1 Cut apples into ⅛" slices (no need to remove the core or peel).

2 Combine the lemon juice and salt, and dip the apple slices into this liquid.

3 Drain the slices in a colander, saving the juice for more dipping.

4 Place the slices on racks placed on cookie sheets in a 200°F oven for up to 6 hours, leaving the oven door open for the first 2–3 hours to allow moisture to escape.

5 The apples are done when they are leathery and not soft (mushy).

6 Allow slices to cool completely; then store in an airtight container.

CHAPTER 2

Gifts for the Body

Make gifts to pamper yourself and your loved ones from readily available materials and herbs from your garden. These products are truly gifts for the senses: tactile, aromatic, healing, and a joy to use. Once you begin to create your own herbal cosmetics, you'll discover the incredible possibilities for beautiful gift presentations — found bottles, old recycled jars relabeled in your own hand, baskets full of homemade sensual products for your friends and yourself. The gifts here can be made in the depth of winter, using dried herbs from your abundant harvest to warm your kitchen and fill your home with the wonderful scents of the summer. These are the kind of gifts that people request over and over: "I'm out of Body Splash." You'll also hear, "When are you going to make more?"

Bath Salts

Great for the skin, bath salts turn a plain, practical bath into a luxurious, relaxing "time out." Alone or mixed with herbs, grains, milk, or any of the additives suggested on page 25, bath salts clean and relax sore muscles, and the aroma helps you forget the stresses of your hectic day. For a milk bath, instead of all bath salts, use half powdered milk and half bath salts.

INGREDIENTS

1 cup bath salts

⅓	cup Epsom salts
⅓	cup sea salt
⅓	cup baking soda
15–20	drops essential oil (see below)

Cleansing Blend

6 drops lavender oil
6 drops grapefruit oil
4 drops juniper oil

Earthy Blend

6 drops sandalwood oil
6 drops patchouli oil
6 drops lavender oil

Refreshing Blend

6 drops rosewood oil
6 drops bergamot oil
4 drops frankincense oil

1 In a large bowl, mix together the salts and soda.

2 Using an eyedropper, add the oils to the salt mixture and stir to combine.

3 Store in clean mason jars with tight-fitting lids to keep salts dry and free-flowing.

4 Use about 1 tablespoon of salts per bath. Add to bath directly under running tap or hang them in a bath bag from the faucet. Use warm water, not hot. Your skin will be more receptive to the healing powers of the bath additives if the water is not hot, and the essential oils will retain their effectiveness longer.

Gift Idea ❧

Make a cloth cover for the mason jar lid to serve double duty as a bath bag. Cut a 5″ diameter circle out of muslin and finish the edge by folding over ¼″ and then ½″ to make a casing, leaving a small opening for the drawstring. Then, using embroidery floss or some other string or cord attached to a small safety pin, thread the draw cord through the casing.

Lid converts to a bag that holds 1 tablespoon of bath salts. Rinse after each use.

Scented Soap Balls

This simple recipe will show you how to transform plain castile or glycerin soap into something wonderful for the skin. Make soaps in small quantities (three balls per batch), so you can experiment readily with scents and offer a mixture of soaps as a gift. You can find lanolin in most pharmacies; special oils are available in health food stores or through herbal mail-order catalogs (see Source List, page 117).

INGREDIENTS

Two 3½-ounce bars unscented castile or glycerin soap, grated

1   tablespoon anhydrous lanolin

1   tablespoon sweet almond, castor, jojoba, or quality vegetable oil

2   tablespoons ground oatmeal or cornmeal

1   tablespoon crushed lavender, rosemary, or peppermint

10   drops essential oil (same scent as flower, or complementary scent)

Vegetable oil for hands

EQUIPMENT

Double boiler
Metal spoon
Waxed paper

1   Melt grated soap, lanolin, and oil in a double boiler until the mixture is a soft, mushy consistency. Stir occasionally while melting.

2   Remove from heat and stir in remaining ingredients.

3   While the soap mixture is cooling, oil your hands. When the soap is cool enough to work, form it into balls. Place the balls on waxed paper to cool.

Healing Gifts ❧

Soap balls make a great gift. When the soap balls are completely hardened, they can be packaged in paper or wrapped in squares of netting and tied with ribbon. Present them in straw-lined (or potpourri-lined) baskets, along with washcloths or loofah sponges. Make some of the other cosmetic products in this chapter, using similar scents, to create a basket of complete bath and skin products for a friend.

Parsley — An Unlikely Medicinal Herb

Did you know that parsley is very beneficial in healing acne, eczema, and psoriasis? It can be infused into water or steeped in witch hazel to make a lotion, or used as a facial steam, with other herbs added to enhance the scent. To make a basic steam, boil 3 cups of distilled water. Remove from heat and add 2 teaspoons dried parsley and 1 teaspoon lavender, rosemary, or mint. Cover the pot and allow it to steep for 5 minutes. Place the pot in a place where you can lean over it safely and sit comfortably for 10 minutes. Place a towel over your head, close your eyes, relax, and steam clean your face!

Herbs and Their Benefits ∾

Herbs can be blended to combine scent with medicinal properties, the list is endless. Or you can make the soap unscented, but with the beneficial grains and fats, for those who have allergies or simply don't care for scented products. Eliminate the essential oils but include the flower infusion to produce a mildly scented soap, not overpowering in any way.

Calendula	Stimulating and healing to the skin
Chamomile	Pineapple scent; astringent and antiseptic
Elderberry	Fruity; stimulating and astringent
Eucalyptus	Minty and refreshing; antiseptic properties
Lavender	Flowery aroma with astringent properties
Lemon, lemon balm, and lemon verbena	Refreshing and cleansing; good for oily skin
Mints	Invigorating and astringent
Rose	Old-fashioned floral scent; relaxing
Sage	Stimulating and antibacterial

Bath Bags

These simple-to-make terry cloth bags can be filled with bath salts, herbs, grated soap, or the cleansing blends described below.

MATERIALS

Makes two bags

Terry cloth washcloth (approximately 12″ x 12″ or yardage*

24″ beaded eyelet trim (the kind with holes to thread ribbon through)

24″ drawstring or ribbon

EQUIPMENT

Scissors

Needle and thread or sewing machine

* You can make these bags using larger pieces of terry cloth instead of washcloths. To adapt the instructions, simply cut the terry cloth 12″ x 6″. Serge or zigzag stitch around all four sides. Then proceed from step 2. Each 12″ x 6″ piece will make one bag.

1 Cut the washcloth in half. (Each half makes one bath bag.)

2 Stitch the eyelet trim to the long finished edge of the washcloth, ½″ in from the edge, stitching close to both edges of the eyelet.

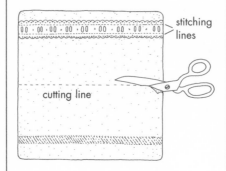

stitching lines

cutting line

3 Fold the cut washcloth in half crosswise, right sides together, and stitch along the two raw edges to form the bag, using a ¼″ to ½″ seam allowance. Make sure that you catch the ends of the eyelet trim in the seam. Clip the corner to eliminate bulk in the bag. If you have a serger, you can serge this seam to finish the edges. (A serger is a sewing machine that does an overedge stitch to prevent raveling.)

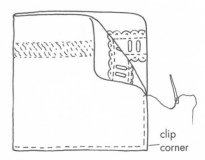

clip corner

4 Turn the bag right-side out and thread the drawstring through the eyelet beads (holes), so that the longer spans are under the eyelet and the drawstring shows between each set of beads. Tie a knot to join the two ends of the drawstring.

5 Repeat for the second half of the washcloth.

To Use

These bags serve a dual purpose — to infuse the bathwater with salt and scents and beneficial grains, and to scrub your skin with the filled terry cloth. Fill a bag with about ½ cup of bath additives, hang it from the faucet as you run the bath, and allow the salts and milk to dissolve and the herbs to infuse your bathwater. Then use the terrycloth scrubber to cleanse your skin. After each use, turn the bag inside out and rinse it well.

Suggestions for Filling the Bags ❧

You can make a premixed blend and keep it in a jar by the tub to refill your bath bag each time, or keep jars of herbs, bath salts, powdered milk, and various grains handy to mix a custom blend each time you bathe. As a general rule, combine 1 part grains to 1 part herbs or bath salts and add soap and/or milk as desired.

- *For a soothing bath:* oatmeal
- *For cleansing dry skin:* ground almonds or sunflower seeds
- *For an abrasive bath to remove grease and grime:* cornmeal
- *For a milk bath:* powdered milk
- *For a relaxing herbal bath:* chamomile, comfrey, lavender, lemon verbena, sassafras, thyme, or vanilla
- *For a stimulating herbal bath:* bay, elder, hops, jasmine, lemon balm, marjoram, patchouli, peppermint, rosemary, savory, or yarrow
- *For a soothing herbal bath:* aloe vera, birch bark, calendula, catnip, comfrey, hyssop, rose, sage
- *For a sudsy scrub:* grated soap

Making Inner Bathbag Packets

Instead of keeping various jars of ingredients in the bathroom, you can make pouches — like tea bags — filled with ready-blended bath additives. These are particularly good as gifts.

MATERIALS

Cheesecloth or sheer sew-in interfacing (not the fusible kind)
String (for drawstring bags) *or*
Sewing machine for sewn pouches

EQUIPMENT

Scissors
Stapler (optional)
Needle and thread or sewing machine (optional)

To make the simplest version, cut 6″ x 6″ squares of fabric. Place ¼–½ cup of salts, herbs, and grains in the center of the square. Gather the edges into a pouch and tie with string. If desired, staple a 1″ x 1″ label to the string end, with ingredients and instructions.

If you like to sew, stitch many small pouches at once by marking a double layer of fabric

Gift Idea ∾

For an unusual housewarming gift, purchase a set of towels with matching washcloths (or find washcloths that match the homeowner's towels). Make one of the washcloths into two bath bags. Include a jar or two of blended bath salts, oatmeal, or herbs, with a note reminding the recipient of the importance of relaxation and occasional pampering. Or fill a gift basket with soaps, a couple of bath bags, and several different inner pouches for stimulating, relaxing, and soothing baths, so your friend can choose ingredients based on the kind of day she's had.

with a wide, then narrow channel, every 3″ and ½″. Stitch along these lines. Then stitch in the other direction every 7″ and 7½″. Cut the fabric halfway between the 7″ and 7½″ stitch lines, and again between the ½″ stitch lines, creating rows of 3″ wide pouches with open tops. Fill each row of pouches and stitch them closed. Cut them apart, label, and use them in gift baskets.

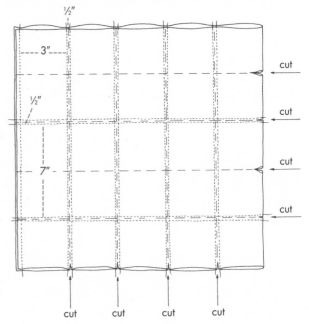

Essential Oil Blends

More and more shops are beginning to carry essential oils. Since they are rather expensive, most people start with one or two scents and gradually add more to their repertoire. Be sure to purchase pure essential oil, not a diluted blend. Please read the safety precautions on essential oils below, before beginning these recipes.

Massage, Bath, or Body Oil: Combine 2 ounces of carrier oil with 25 drops of essential oil. For bath oil, Turkey Red oil is the best carrier. It's a processed castor oil that will diffuse into the water instead of floating on the top.

Personal Perfume: Combine ½ ounce alcohol (Evercleer or Vodka) or jojoba oil with 10–15 drops essential oil.

Fragrant Spritz: Combine 16 ounces of water with 20–30 drops essential oil in a spray bottle. Use this spritz as an air freshener or a body spray.

Body Lotion: Combine 8 ounces of unscented body lotion or aloe vera gel with 20–30 drops of essential oil. Add a capsule of vitamin E oil to increase the lotion's healing powers.

Liquid Soap: To 4 ounces of unscented liquid soap, add 20 drops of essential oil.

Note: Use hand-decorated containers when presenting these fragrant blends as gifts (see page 35 for suggestions.)

Essential Oil Safety ∾

Essential oils are always blended into a *carrier* (an unscented oil), since used full strength they can irritate the skin. Common carriers are sweet almond, grape seed, apricot kernel, and jojoba oil. Adding 10 percent wheat germ or avocado oil to the carrier provides extra vitamins, minerals, and proteins to the finished skin product.

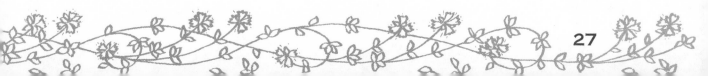

Herbal Body Splashes

Body splashes — also known as toners, astringents, aftershaves, table waters, and toilet waters — are easy to make. Steep herbs and flowers in water or witch hazel to release the scents into the liquid. These splashes are completely natural and inexpensive to use for testing different blends from your garden. Tincture of benzoin is used for its astringent and preserving properties. Glycerin is an effective nongreasy moisturizer.

Floral Table Water

INGREDIENTS

2   cups water
½   cup rose petals
½   cup lavender flowers
1   tablespoon thyme
Peel of ½ an orange, sliced
1   teaspoon cloves
Essential oil of rose or lavender
Tincture of benzoin and glycerin
    (optional)
Cheesecloth

1 Boil 2 cups of water and add flowers, herbs, and/or fruit. Cover and allow to steep for 30 minutes.

2 Strain through cheesecloth and test by smell. For a strong scent without adding essential oil, after straining the first time, reheat the same liquid and add more of the same herbs and flowers. Follow the steeping procedure again, and this will produce a more concentrated water. Add 5–10 drops of rose oil or lavender oil, if you like a strong scent.

3 Add 10–15 drops of tincture of benzoin (optional).

4 Add 2 tablespoons glycerin (optional).

5 Store in an airtight container. Label with contents and date.

Herbal Toner

Mix equal parts of each of the following:
- thyme, mint, and sage
- lavender and sage
- mint, lemon balm, lavender, and rosemary
- rosemary, mint, cinnamon, cloves, and citrus peel

Combine with:
- Witchhazel (enough to cover herbs and flowers)

Store in a widemouth jar for at least 2 weeks, shaking frequently then strain and bottle. For each 2 cups of liquid, 15 drops of tincture of benzoin may be added. For a stronger scent, add 5–6 drops of essential oil per cup of witch hazel.

Herbal Lip Balm

This is a fun and novel project to make at home. Add flavored oils to tailor the balm to your own tastes; if you want some color, just add some old lipstick to the mixture. For kids with chapped lips, make a lip balm in their favorite flavor, and they'll be sure to remember to use it.

INGREDIENTS

Makes about ⅓ cup (enough to fill 4–6 tiny lip balm jars)

- 5–6 tablespoons sweet almond, jojoba, castor or quality vegetable oil, or a blend of almond, coconut oil, and cocoa butter
- 1 tablespoon beeswax (white or golden)
- 2 teaspoons honey
- ½ tube (colored, moisturizing) lipstick (optional)
- 10 drops essential oil

EQUIPMENT

Double boiler
4–6 one or two ounce jars, or 1 four ounce jar, with lids

1 In the top of a double boiler, melt the oil and beeswax. Remove from heat.

2 Stir in the honey and blend well.

3 If you want a tinted lip balm, add the lipstick while the mixture is still hot. Or divide the mixture in half and color only part of it. Stir until melted.

4 Continue stirring as the mixture cools to the consistency of petroleum jelly.

5 Add the essential oil (flavoring) when the mixture is almost cool.

6 Pour into small jars with lids. One to two ounce sample jam and mustard jars are ideal for this use. You can also use empty film cans.

Variations: Popular flavors for these lip balms are various mints, citrus oils, apple, cherry, peach, and other fruits. Tea tree oil is often recommended for treatment of cold sores. For a more exotic taste, try vanilla or coconut oil. For flavors with the kind of "zing" kids really like, use synthetic candy flavorings, available in candymaking supply stores and pharmacies. Increase the amount of honey slightly, but if you add too much, your kids will lick the balm off their lips because it tastes so good!

Dream Pillow

Herbal pillows have been used for centuries to help people fall asleep. This pillow contains hops, a known sedative with a less-than-pleasant smell so we add aromatic herbs and flowers to the mix. The pillow cover is easy to clean and an inner pouch allows you to freshen the herbs.

MATERIALS

12″ x 24″ piece of decorative fabric (for pillow cover)

1 yard lace trim, at least 1″ wide

12″ x 24″ piece of muslin (for inner pouch)

¼ cup dried lemon verbena leaves

¼ cup dried rose petals

¼ cup dried chamomile flowers

¼ cup dried rosemary or lavender

15 drops rose or lavender essential oil

¼ cup large pieces of orrisroot

1 cup dried hops flowers

EQUIPMENT

Needle and thread or sewing machine

Iron

Quart jar

SEWING THE COVER

1 On the wrong side of the pillow cover fabric, with a pencil draw a 10″ circle as close to the edge of the fabric as possible. This is the front of the pillow cover. Cut it out.

2 Fold the remaining fabric in half. Draw half a 10″ circle, with a 1½″ tab extension. Cut out the two pieces for the backs of the pillow cover.

3 Turn under ½″ on each edge of the tab extensions and press on the pillow cover backs. Stitch them ⅛″ in from the inner edge.

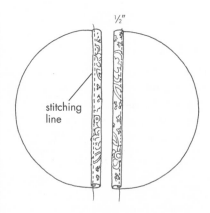

½″

stitching line

4 Baste the lace trim to the front of the front pillow cover, ¼″ in from the edge, with the finished lace edge toward the center of the pillow.

5 Pin the pillow cover backs to the pillow cover front, lining up the edges of the circles and overlapping the inner tab edges of the back cover (these will form the envelope opening in which to insert the herb pouch). Stitch around the entire edge of the circle, using a ½" seam allowance. Turn right-side out and iron flat.

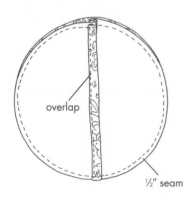

overlap

½" seam

SEWING THE INNER POUCH

6 Fold muslin in half and draw a 9" circle. Cut out circles.

7 Sew pouch pieces together, ¼" from outer edge, backstitching at the start and finish. Leave a 2"–3" opening to insert the herbs. Turn right-side out and press flat.

ASSEMBLING THE PILLOW

8 Mix the floral potpourri ingredients (lemon verbena, rose petals, chamomile, and rosemary or lavender) a week or two ahead so that the oil and orrisroot have a chance to mingle. Put mixture in a quart jar with the orrisroot on top, and drop the oil onto the orrisroot. Shake mixture periodically.

9 Combine the floral potpourri with the hops. Insert this into the inner pouch, either by hand or with a funnel. By hand, sew the pouch closed.

10 Insert the pouch into the pillow cover and adjust the herbs as flat as possible.

Herbal Lore: Sedatives ∿

St.-John's-wort, valerian, and wormwood all have excellent sedative properties. Unfortunately, they are quite unpleasant to the smell.

Catnip, lavender, lemon balm, lemon verbena, and sweet woodruff — all of which smell great — have mild sedative powers, so consider adding these to your pillow if you have them in your garden. If you use catnip or valerian in your herbal mixture and share your home with cats, watch out for your pillow: Cats love these herbs!

Note: These pillows are not intended to be your primary sleeping pillow; they are small and somewhat lumpy. Place them beside or underneath the bed pillow to impart their herbal magic.

Eye Relaxation Bag

It's amazing that such a simple object has become so popular in recent years, but its success is based on the fact that it works! The flax seed and lavender filling has healing properties that relax and relieve headaches. This bag is designed to cover the forehead and eyes. You can cool it in the freezer or heat it in the microwave.

MATERIALS

Tightly woven cotton fabric,
  10″ x 10″
½ **cup flax seed**
½ **cup dried lavender flowers**

EQUIPMENT

Ruler
Chalk or pencil
Needle and thread or sewing
  machine
Canning funnel

1 Fold the fabric in half, right sides together, and press flat.

2 Using a ruler and chalk or pencil, draw the eye bag shape onto the fabric. *Note:* The basic dimensions are 5″ x 10″. Find the center point along the top and bottom of the rectangle.

Draw the center line. Locate a point 1½″ up from the bottom and make a mark. Locate points 2″ on each side of the bottom center point. Draw a curved line connecting the upper (bridge of the nose) point to the two lower points.

3 Pin the halves of the folded piece together and cut them out.

4 Stitch around the eye bag, leaving a 2″–3″ opening along the top edge, but not at a corner. Backstitch at the start and finish of the sewing, so that the bag will not begin to unravel as you fill it.

5 Turn the bag right-side out and iron it. You may need to use a straight pin to pull the corners out completely.

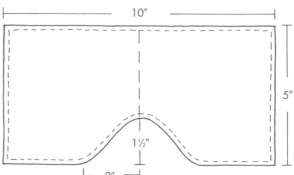

Cutting and stitching diagram

6 Mix together the flax and lavender. If you prefer an unscented bag, use 1 cup of flax and no lavender. The flax seeds contain healing linseed oil, and will stay cool for a long time. The lavender has natural powers of relaxation and adds an old-fashioned aroma.

7 Using a canning funnel — or any funnel with a large spout — fill the bag with the mixture. Pin the bag closed, carefully folding in the seam allowance to match the existing seams.

8 By hand, stitch the bag closed.

Eye Treatment Tea Bags

While the eye relaxation bag is reusable, and is predominantly used for headaches, the following "tea bag" treatments soothe tired, irritated eyes. They make a nice gift for someone who does a lot of close work. The design has been adapted from *Scented Treasures* (see page 124).

MATERIALS

Makes 16 eye bags

2   10½″ x 10½″ pieces of muslin
4   ounces chamomile, catnip, elderflowers, eyebright, fennel, lavender, or orange pekoe tea

EQUIPMENT

Ruler
Soft pencil or chalk
Scissors or pinking shears
Needle and thread

1 Using a ruler and a soft pencil or chalk, on both pieces of muslin mark off 2″ squares with ½″ seam allowances around each one.

2 Carefully place 1 teaspoon of coarse-cut herbs, seeds, tea, or flowers in the center of each square.

3 Place the second piece of muslin over the first and carefully pin between each square.

4 Sew the squares shut. With a scissors or pinking shears, cut between the stitch lines to separate the bags.

TO USE

Place two bags in a saucer. Pour 1 tablespoon of boiling water over them. Cover with another saucer and allow to infuse until cool. Gently squeeze out the excess water and apply to the eyelids for 15 minutes.

For alternative methods, see pages 14–15 and the Bath Bag Inner Pouches, page 26.

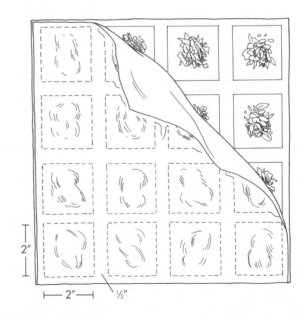

Herbal Hand Cream

I've played around with this recipe a bit, in search of a salve that would moisturize and heal my carpenter husband's hands after a day working with wood, solvents, and abrasives. He prefers it without the essential oil; scented or unscented, though, this cream restores moisture and oils to hands that are sore and dried out by the elements.

INGREDIENTS

Makes about 4 ounces

- 2 **tablespoons water infused with ¼ cup of dried calendula petals**
- 2 **tablespoons beeswax (white or golden)**
- 2 **ounces anhydrous lanolin**
- ⅜ **cup sweet almond or olive oil**
- 1 **capsule of vitamin E oil**
- 15–20 **drops essential oil, if scent is desired (rose, lavender, or other florals)**

EQUIPMENT

Small pot
Double boiler
Wire whisk
Clean jar with lid

1 Make the calendula infusion. Crush the calendula petals in about ¼ cup of water. Bring the mixture to a boil; then turn off the heat. Allow it to steep, covered, until it is cool.

2 Melt the beeswax and lanolin in the top of a double boiler, over simmering water. Remove the top of the double boiler.

3 Strain the calendula petals from the infused water; then add 2 tablespoons of the water to the wax/lanolin mixture. Whisk. The mix should start to become creamy.

4 Add the almond or olive oil. Puncture the gel capsule filled with vitamin E, and squeeze the vitamin E oil into the mixture. Continue whisking frequently as you allow the mixture to cool. As it cools, it will become thicker and creamier.

5 While the cream is still warm but not hot, add the essential oil (if desired). This can be any scent you like; the calendula petals have very little scent, and are included mainly for their healing properties.

6 Pour the cream into a jar and allow it to cool completely before capping. Label the finished product.

Bottles, Jars, and Tubs for Making Decorative Gifts

Finding jars just when you decide to make creams and lotions can be frustrating. I'm always on the lookout for interesting bottles, jars, and tubs with lids. Sample mustard and jam jars are great for lip balms and small gifts of massage oil. Empty herb and spice jars hold 2–4 ounces of liquid lotion.

I keep a box of assorted jars and bottles in an out-of-the-way cabinet, and when I start making concoctions, I sterilize them to be sure they're really clean.

Even a jar with a manufacturer's label can be recycled into a decorative container for herbal cosmetics. Some forms of decoration prevent you from washing the jars, so sterilize them before starting your artistic endeavor. The herbal cosmetics in this book do not require refrigeration and are unlikely to go rancid, so it is unnecessary to pour the finished product into a hot jar just out of boiling water. Once the sterilization is done, you can take the time to paint or decoupage the containers.

Here are some ideas:

- *Glass jars with printed metal lids* can be turned into decorative containers by painting the outside of the lid with enamel paint. The little jars that are used for pimentos and other concentrated condiments make great candidates for this process. Be sure not to get any paint on the inside of the lid, where the rubberized seal is located. If you collect many of these jars, paint several jar lids at one time, so you have them ready when you need them, and then either paint the contents' label on the lid or use an adhesive label on the glass jar itself.

- *Plastic or glass tubs* (the kind that cold cream comes in) can be painted or collaged. Clean and sterilize them thoroughly. If they are plastic, use medium-grit sandpaper to "rough up" the outer surface of the jar and the lid so that paints and glues will adhere.

- *For decoupage*, use products designed specifically for this process, such as Mod-Podge, or white glue thinned with a little water plus an acrylic finish for the final coat. I keep a folder of interesting magazine and catalog clippings for this purpose. For a jar of fragrant cream, use clippings of herbs to match the scent of the contents. If you know in advance what you will be putting in the jar, you can collage the words onto the jar surface. Brush the jar with the glue product, stick the clippings as you want them arranged, and brush over them again. You can also combine this technique with painting, but wait for the glue to be completely dry before you paint. Then apply a final coat of finish.

CHAPTER 3

Decorative Herbal Gifts

This chapter contains projects that use herbs, and painted images of them, as decorative motifs on practical items such as containers and stationery. You'll spend hours of enjoyment embellishing paper, ceramic, and glass.

Having good source material available makes painting botanical subjects much easier. Use gardening manuals, seed and gift catalogs, seed packets, encyclopedias, and any other print material with good illustrations as references for your designs. You don't have to be a trained artist, and you don't have to reproduce a botanical drawing exactly — simply capturing the leaf shape, the curve of a stem, the color of a flower can be quite pleasing to the eye. Leaves and flowers can be used as stencils or stamps and photos can be traced. Often the simplest designs are the most appreciated.

Many of these projects employ techniques that are outlined in greater detail on pages 106–115; please read that section before you begin.

Stamped Photo Frames

Transform plain wooden photo frames into personalized gifts using simple homemade stamps and paints. Look for relatively flat frames — I find interesting ones at junk stores and garage sales. If you know ahead of time what you will be framing, consider matching some of the colors in the frame design to create a coordinated art piece.

MATERIALS

Wooden picture frame, flat
Sandpaper, medium-grit
Acrylic paints
Acrylic gloss, medium
Picture wire

EQUIPMENT

Flat brush, 1″–2″ width
Small round brush
Sponges or foam rubber
Palette or plastic plates
Kitchen scissors or mat knife
Newspaper or other scrap paper

1 Prepare the frame surface. Although acrylics will adhere to any surface, I find it beneficial to "rough up" the surface with some medium-grit sandpaper, particularly if the frame has a glossy finish when you begin.

2 Decide whether you want an undercoat of color, or if the existing frame color is acceptable to you. With the flat brush, paint whatever background color you choose. Allow it to dry thoroughly.

CUTTING THE STAMPS

3 If you want a stamped shape that shows the sponge holes, choose a plain kitchen sponge. If you prefer a more solid stamped shape, use foam rubber (available in craft and sewing stores) — it's denser and doesn't have

irregular holes in it. Draw the shape onto the surface of the sponge. Using scissors or a sharp kitchen knife, cut out the shapes. For this project, I have chosen a basic pansy silhouette and leaf.

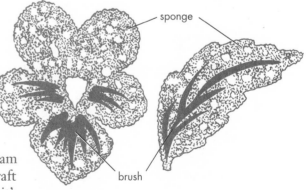

sponge

brush

STAMPING

4 Mix the paint colors on the palette or plate with some acrylic medium. This will thin and extend the paint (it will stay liquid longer with the medium, and will not be runny, as it would if you added water).

5 Holding the stamp flat, dip it into the paint. Test the stamp on scrap paper to determine how much paint will make a solid, but not blotchy, shape. You may need to blot the stamp each time you ink it, to achieve the optimal paint quantity. (This scrap paper can make terrific wrapping paper!) Stamp the frame as you wish. Random patterns or concentrations of flowers at the corners are lovely. You can mix colors directly on the stamp, making a leaf dark green at the base and lighter green at the tip.

6 When the basic shapes are to your liking, allow the paints to dry thoroughly. Now, with the small round brush, paint details — the yellow centers of the pansies or the veins of the leaves, for example.

7 When all of the paints are dry, finish the frame with a smooth coat (or two) of acrylic gloss medium.

Mounting Your Art

Mat cutting takes practice, but with a good metal ruler, sharp blades, and a flat cutting surface, anyone can do it. These instructions are for straight-cut mat edges.

MATERIALS

Mat board

Cutting surface (a second piece of board or a cork or rubber surface)

Metal ruler, longer than the longest length you need to cut

Mat or X-acto knife with a sharp, new blade

1 Measure dimensions of the area inside the frame, where the mat slips in. Cut the outer dimensions of the mat ⅛″ smaller than the frame in length and width. Using the ruler, draw these dimensions on the back of the mat board.

2 Measure your artwork and determine where you want its outer borders to be and how much mat will be visible through the glass of the frame. While there is no real standard, many mats are 2½″ around the top and sides and 3″ at the bottom.

3 Measure in from the sides of the mat to mark off the mat's inner borders, keeping all lines square.

4 When cutting, always hold the ruler against the mat to protect it, so that if you slip with the knife, your accidental cut will slice outside of the mat itself. This means that you will be turning the mat as you cut it. When you cut the inner lines, position the ruler so that a slip of the knife will slice the inner (discarded) piece of mat.

5 Begin by cutting the outer edges of the mat. To cut, hold the ruler firmly with your non-dominant hand. Cut on the wrong side of the mat board. Starting at the top, hold the blade perpendicular to the ruler, push the blade exactly into the corner, and run it firmly and smoothly down the entire length of the cut. Resituate the knife in the same groove and

repeat the cutting until you have severed the board. With a sharp knife, two passes should be enough.

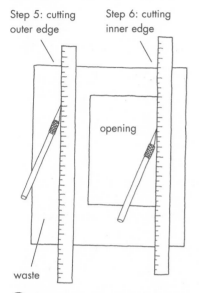

Step 5: cutting outer edge

Step 6: cutting inner edge

opening

waste

6 After cutting the mat's outer edges, cut the inner "frame": Place the knife blade exactly at the corner and cut down exactly to the adjacent corner. Any slipping past the corner will show on the front of the mat.

7 If there are rough spots, gently smooth the inside edges of the mat with an emery board.

8 To mount the artwork: Artwork is hung from the top of the mat, so that it can flex over

time and climate changes. Put a piece of masking tape on the upper back edge of the artwork, adhesive side facing up. Place the mat over the art. When it is situated properly, push down on the tape. Then, turn the mat over and secure the tape well, along the top edge only.

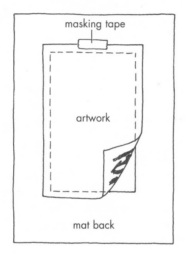

masking tape

artwork

mat back

ASSEMBLING THE FRAME

Put the glass in first, followed by the matted art. If the frame requires cardboard or foam board to fill it, this goes in next. Then, secure the back, using whatever method the frame requires. Run picture wire across the back, and hang it!

Decorating Possibilities ∾

∾ Stamp the mat to match or complement the frame.

∾ To mount pressed flowering herbs on the mat, carefully brush thinned white glue on the back of the flowers and place them with tweezers.

∾ Cut multiple mats of different colors, each with slightly smaller inner frame than the previous, to leave small inner borders around the art.

Painted Vinegar Bottles

You can turn plain vinegar bottles into decorative decanters with a little paint and your imagination. Choose smooth-finish glass bottles, with or without lids (you can always cork them), to provide a paintable surface. Sterilize them with boiling water and dry thoroughly, and you're ready to begin. (See Herbal Vinegars *project, page 16.)*

MATERIALS
Glass bottle
Newspaper
Masking tape
Oil-based enamel paints (these are
   glossy and require no finish coat)
Thinner (as indicated on the paints)

EQUIPMENT
Glass tray (for mixing paints)
Glass jar with lid, for thinner
Variety of brushes

1 Sketch your design on paper, and practice painting it on the newspaper.

2 You can paint the bottle while it's standing upright. For more control while painting on a flat surface, make a "cradle" for the bottle to prevent it from rolling. Roll up two wads of newspaper, which will sit on either side of the bottle. Tape

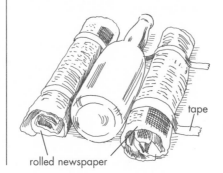

rolled newspaper

tape

them to the table so that the space between them cradles the bottle as it is lying down, and holds it up as far off the paper as you need it to be. If you are going to paint both sides of the bottle, wait until the first side dries before turning it over.

3 Paint a "blotch" on the bottle. This is a base coat of paint — white or any other color — in the shape of your finished design. It coats the glass and gives an opaque surface on which to paint your design. (You need a clear idea of what you are going to paint in order to know what shape to make the blotch.)

Step 3:
"Blotch"

Step 5:
Finished design

4 When the blotch is dry, sketch in pencil or paint free-hand directly on it. If you are doing any wording, it helps to sketch it out first. To trace the design from a sketch, tape it to the bottle and slip carbon paper underneath it. Trace through both layers with a pencil or ball-point pen.

5 Paint the design, allowing each color to dry before painting on top of it. If you want colors to blend, paint wet-on-wet.

Herbal Liqueurs

These bottles make excellent containers for herbal liqueurs and cordials. Here's a basic recipe and some variations:

INGREDIENTS

- 4 **cups vodka**
- 2 **pints fruit, such as berries, pears, apricots, citrus, and zest, and/or**
- 2 **tablespoons of herbs and spices, such as ginger, anise, and/or**
- ¼ **cup herbs, such as thyme or mint, and/or**
- 1 **cup fragrant leaves or flowers, such as lemon verbena, rose geranium leaves**
- 1 **cup sugar**
- ½ **cup water**

EQUIPMENT

1 gallon glass jar with airtight lid
Strainer
Coffee filter
Clean bottles

1 Combine vodka, fruit, and herbs in a glass jar with airtight lid. Steep in a cool, dark place for 1 month, stirring and crushing the fruit and herbs weekly.

2 Strain the liquid, crushing all the juice out of the fruit. Strain the juice through a coffee filter.

3 Boil the sugar and water together until the sugar has dissolved, and allow it to cool. Add it slowly to the liqueur, tasting after each small addition. When the liqueur is done steeping and the taste is right, sterilize the bottles and then use a funnel to pour the liqueur into them. Age for another month before serving.

Painted Ceramic Pots

Terra-cotta pots come in many shapes and sizes, and, when decorated, can be used as herb planters, candleholders, or, lettered with greetings or garden quotes, containers for garden paraphernalia. Avoid completely covering the pot with paint which inhibits air and water circulation.

MATERIALS

Unglazed terra-cotta (red clay) pots or other containers
Ceramic paint or acrylics

EQUIPMENT

Flat brushes for large areas
Small round brushes for detail
Sponges (optional)
Plastic containers or plates for mixing/thinning paints

1 Clean and dry the pots thoroughly.

2 Using the flat brush, paint bands of color around the pot, or cut herbal shapes out of sponges and sponge print basic silhouettes onto the pot. For example, paint or sponge the shape of a mint leaf. When the basic shape is dry, use brighter shades of appropriate colors to paint in the details.

3 If you are using the pots for candleholders, paint the inside with metallic gold paint to produce a reflective glow.

Note: The hole in the bottom of the pot should be filled with clay, putty, or covered with a disk or saucer (from the inside) to prevent wax from seeping out.

Variations: Create pretty pots for a window herb garden by painting a band of white around each pot and lettering the name of an herb onto the band. Present the pot already planted or with a corresponding seed packet inside.

Decorate smooth rocks using the same technique. Coat with several layers of varnish for outdoor use.

Herb-Printed Calendar

You and your children can make this calendar throughout the year, as you harvest the month's bounty, or all at one time, using herbs and leaves to decorate each month's display. See pages 113 – 115 for techniques. Each page is made separately and then mounted to the calendar blank; this project requires several steps to complete.

MATERIALS

Seven 8½″ x 11″ manila file folders
  (they'll actually measure larger)
Yarn or twine
25 sheets 8½″ x 11″ quality bond or
  rag paper
Fine-point marker, black
Water-based printing inks
Herb leaves and flowers for printing
Tube watercolors, for embellishing
  the prints
Rubber cement

EQUIPMENT

Scissors or sharp knife
Large needle and carpet thread or
  deep-throated stapler
Hole punch
Metal ruler
Glass or plastic sheet (for rolling
  out ink)

Paper towels or blank newsprint
Brayer (roller) or dabber

MAKING THE CALENDAR BLANK

1 Cut the tabs off the manila folders.

2 Place the 7 folders on top of one another, with the folds lined up.

3 Use a running stitch to attach the folders to each other. Work back over the stitch line to the center of the folders (at the 5½″ point), and make a loop on the outside of the folders, for hanging the calendar.

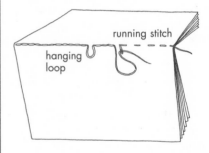

Note: If sewing the folders seems too difficult, use the hole punch to make two holes along the fold line of each folder, located 3″ in from the edge. Then, use yarn or twine to tie all seven folders together. If you have a deep-throated stapler, simply staple the folders together, and then staple a loop to the outside for hanging.

Making the Calendar Pages

See the sidebar (page 45) on how to make and use a raised ruler.

Mark off a month grid lightly in pencil on each of 12 sheets of paper as follows (if desired, you can follow steps 4–6 once, and then photocopy it 12 times):

4 Measure in ¼" from the 8½" edge and mark off 1½" columns across the page. You should have seven 1½" columns and ¼" margins on each edge.

5 Measure in ¼" from the bottom 11" edge and mark off five 1½" rows up the page. Then mark a ½" row, and finish with a ¼" margin. You should have five 1½" rows, with a ¼" margin on each edge, and a ½" space below the margin at the top of each page, for the days of the week.

6 Using the raised ruler, hold the fine-point marker perpendicular to the ruler and draw the margins around the page. Now draw all of the row and column lines, ending each line at the margin line.

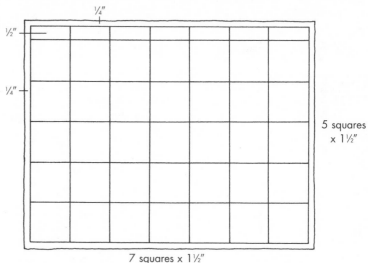

¼"

½"

¼"

5 squares x 1½"

7 squares x 1½"

7 Write the days of the week into the ½" slots at the top of each column.

8 Using a calendar for the upcoming year, copy the dates and corresponding days of the week onto each month's page. If you like, write significant holidays or birthdays onto the appropriate pages. For a gardening gift, indicate planting or harvesting dates.

Nature Printing the Calendar Months

Kids will love this part of the project. Using seasonal leaves, flowers, and fruit, you will be decorating one sheet of paper for each month.

9 Choose the plant materials for the month of January. Prepare the palette (see pages 114–115 for techniques) with one or several colors of ink, thinned with extender, with a brayer or dabber.

10 You have a choice here: You can compose the entire page at once or print each leaf separately. If you print each separately, ink one leaf, situate it on the page, cover it with a paper towel, and rub it with your hand or the back of a spoon to

transfer the ink to the page. To print the entire page at once, be sure to extend the ink enough to keep it wet and workable during the time it takes you to do the layout. Then, lay toweling on the sheet and either roll the entire page with a clean brayer or make a walking press setup (see page 114 for technique).

11 Make a page for each month, and a 13th page for the front of the calendar. You may want to embellish the prints with watercolors, once they are somewhat dry, using small brushes. You can add shades of yellow to an all-green leaf, for example. Use a fine-point marker for detail work and to write the names of the different plants.

12 Inks take several weeks to cure fully. Allow the printed pages to set, not touching other pages, for about a month before mounting into the calendar.

PUTTING IT ALL TOGETHER

Now that you have your folders made into calendar format, each month drawn on a separate sheet and a page of nature prints for each month, you are ready to assemble the finished product.

13 Measure in from the edges of each page of the calendar to center each 8½″ x 11″ sheet. Make light pencil marks at each corner to guide you in the gluing process.

14 Cover the file folder with rubber cement, using the brush provided and working within the guidelines you have marked. Allow this glue to become tacky. Meanwhile, brush the cement around the edge of the back of the printed page, making a 1″ border of glue all around. (Putting cement on both surfaces allows rubber cement to act like contact cement; it will form a permanent bond.) Avoid saturating the printed page with adhesive; you don't want the glue to show through the print.

15 Carefully place the sheet on the file folder, within the corner guidelines. When it is in place, rub every inch of the print into place. Repeat this for all 25 sheets.

Arts and Crafts Hint ∾

Using pens to mark lines against a metal straightedge can be frustrating if the ink smears when you move the ruler. To avoid this, make a raised ruler. All you need is a metal ruler (12″ is a good size), 4 pennies, and some masking tape. Carefully tape the pennies, evenly spaced, down the back of the ruler. This will raise the ruler about ¹⁄₁₆″ and eliminate smearing the ink under the metal. When you use this ruler for measuring, remember to keep your pencil straight up and down. Since the ruler is not directly on the paper, your measurements can be thrown off by the distance between the ruler and the paper, especially if you are working at an angle.

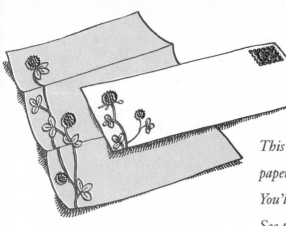

Herb-Printed Note Cards

This project will show you how to create beautiful stationery using fine rag paper or plain bond paper, which can be fed through your computer printer. You'll also find instructions for making and printing matching envelopes. See pages 113–115 for nature printing techniques.

MATERIALS
Typing or rag paper, any size
Envelopes
Small pressed leaves
Paper towels or unprinted newsprint

EQUIPMENT
Metal ruler
Stamp pads (any colors)
Tweezers
Scissors

1 If you have chosen rag paper, the best way to cut it is to tear it. Determine what size you want for your cards or stationery, mark the paper, and hold a metal ruler against the line. Pull up gently to tear a straight but ragged line, which is the traditional finished edge for rag papers.

2 To print stationery with matching envelopes, you will need to ink the leaves on both sides. Use tweezers to move the leaf on and off of the stamp pad, and to place it on the paper.

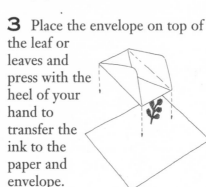

3 Place the envelope on top of the leaf or leaves and press with the heel of your hand to transfer the ink to the paper and envelope.

4 If you are printing on one surface only, simply ink the underside of each leaf, use tweezers to move the leaf carefully to the paper, cover leaf with paper towel or unprinted paper, and rub with the heel of your hand to make the print. You can print many leaves at once.

5 Repeat the printing process until you are satisfied with your stationery, carefully removing the printed leaves with the tweezers and being sure not to smudge the wet ink.

6 Allow the ink to dry completely before using the stationery.

Making Your Own Envelopes

Use the same paper as you used for your cards. Buying paper in 24" x 36" sheets will make this venture more affordable.

1 Measure the card you wish to insert in an envelope. Add at least ¼" to each dimension for the basic envelope size.

2 With a pencil, draw a rectangle the size of the envelope, with a border around it large enough to fit the flaps, which are as wide as the envelope.

3 Draw lines out from the bottom of the rectangle the same length as the rectangle itself. Angle the flaps, A and B, down from the top edge of the rectangle, so that they finish 1" above the bottom edge.

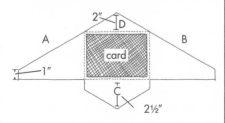

4 Draw flap C so that its sides are 1" straight from each edge, then angle to a point 2½" from edge of rectangle.

5 The closure flap (D) is a triangle at least 2" deep.

6 Cut along the outline of the resulting shape. If you want a ragged edge on the envelope closure flap, tear it carefully.

7 To assemble the envelope, use rubber cement. Fold flap B over flap A and glue them together. Put glue on the inside of flap C, fold and glue to flaps A/B. Put the card in the envelope and fold down the closure flap to seal in the card. Use rubber cement, or make your own mucilage (see at right).

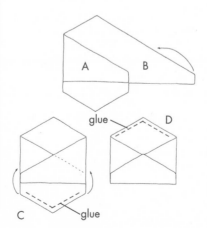

Making Your Own Mucilage

This homemade recipe for old-fashioned mucilage can be painted onto envelope flaps and remoistened when you want to seal them. (It makes great kids' homemade stickers. And it's lemon flavored, so it's not too yucky!) Use only on regular bond or kraft paper, as mucilage is absorbed into rag paper.

MATERIALS
Makes ¼ cup of mucilage (enough for a few dozen envelopes)

   3 **tablespoons white vinegar**
   2 **packets unflavored gelatin**
1½ **teaspoons lemon extract**
Bond or kraft paper envelopes

EQUIPMENT
Saucepan
Small brush

1 Boil vinegar. Add gelatin and stir to dissolve.

2 Add lemon extract and stir.

To use, brush the mucilage onto paper. Allow it to dry. Moisten it to affix to another surface.

Handmade Paper

Papermaking can be very complex, but this simple technique will enable you to use readily available materials and equipment to make beautiful handmade paper. Once you've mastered the basics, experiment with herbs, flowers, and other additives (suggestions are given after the basic instructions).

MATERIALS

5 facial tissues or 3 paper napkins
2 cups of boiling water
4 pieces of cotton fabric, larger
  than the frame

EQUIPMENT

Pitcher, about 1 quart
Tray or cookie sheet
Embroidery hoop or small
  picture frame
Blender
Iron and ironing board
Sponge
Rolling pin

1 Work near a sink or bucket. Tear the paper into strips and place the strips into the pitcher. Add the boiling water and allow to steep for 10 minutes.

2 Lay a piece of cotton fabric on the tray, making sure that the material is flat and the tray level.

3 Position the frame in the center of the fabric.

4 Mix the paper and water in the blender for 5 seconds to form a creamy pulp. Turn on the iron to medium heat.

5 Quickly pour the pulp into the frame and shake the tray to disperse the fibers. Use the sponge to mop up any water outside the frame. Lay a piece of cotton fabric onto the pulp and frame to absorb even more of the water, and continue mopping with the sponge until most of the water has been removed.

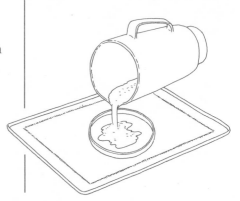

6 Lift the fabric off and carefully remove the frame. Put a new piece of fabric over the paper pulp, and gently roll over the "sandwich" with the rolling pin. Carefully remove this layer of fabric and replace it with a dry one. Smooth it down, and begin to iron it until the fabric feels dry. Turn the sandwich over, and peel the wet fabric off the back. Replace it with the dry fabric and iron until it feels dry. Continue ironing the fabric and paper until the paper feels bone dry.

7 Remove the top piece of fabric, and use a knife to peel the paper from the lower piece of fabric.

Scenting Paper

You can use the same method for dyeing or combine the scented herbs and flowers with the pulp at the blending stage of the mixing process. Your paper will have the color, scent, and texture of the plant material in it.

Naturally Dyed Paper

Instead of adding plain boiling water to the paper strips, make naturally dyed liquid first. Pour 2 cups of boiling water over 1 cup of plant or vegetable matter. Allow to steep until cool. Strain out the plant materials, reboil the liquid, and add it to the paper strips.

Plants and vegetables for dyeing ❧

Onion skins	Yellow
Beets	Pink
Red cabbage	Pink
Daffodils	Bright yellow
Delphiniums	Blue/green
Spinach	Green

Mottled Color

Along with tissues and napkins, most uncoated paper can be "pulped" and re-formed into interesting blends of paper. Try adding egg cartons, colored tissue paper, construction paper, dryer lint, bits of fiber and thread, glitter, plant leaves, and fibers. Avoid printed newspaper and magazines — the ink causes problems. Any paper that is more substantial than the tissues and napkins in the basic instructions will need to soak more than 10 minutes. Tear the paper into small pieces (1"–2"), pour boiling water over the pieces, and allow to stand from 2 hours to overnight before blending.

Textured Paper

You can add seeds, stems, and petals to the pulp just before you pour it. These will be placed randomly in the sheet of paper, depending on how they pour out of the pitcher. You can also embed objects in the paper, and repour a thin layer over them to hold them in the fiber mat. Pour a sheet of paper, quickly lay some pressed rose petals on top, and pour a thin layer of pulp over them. They will show through a film of white fiber.

Homemade paper is usually thicker and more irregular than purchased paper. Be prepared to create some unusual gifts with it!

Embossed or Cast Paper

You can make paper with textures or patterns cast into its surface by designing the surface into which you pour.

MATERIALS AND EQUIPMENT

Paper pulp
Net bag or sieve
Wooden frame
Wood board
Wool/felt or wool blanket cut into several pieces or newspaper
Objects to create texture, like seed pods, bulky flowers, interesting bark or woody stems, etc.
Nonstick baking spray
Rolling pin

1 Prepare the pulp by soaking the paper pieces. Pour them into a net bag or sieve to make a thicker pulp, but don't let the pulp become unpourable.

2 Lay the frame onto the wooden board. Lay the wooden board on absorbent wool felt, wool blanket, or newspaper, which is larger than the board. The frame and board should lie flat and flush against each other.

3 Arrange the objects inside the frame. Spray the entire surface with nonstick spray.

4 Pour the pulp into the frame, covering the objects. Add pulp by hand to any high points that may not have gotten covered in the pour.

5 Place a piece of fabric or felt over the pulp and press down gently, mopping up water as it seeps out. Gently compress and firm the pulp. Peel back the fabric, and add pulp if you have any weak or bare spots. Replace the felt with a dry piece and continue pressing — with your hands and then with a rolling pin — to remove as much water as possible.

6 Remove the felt and place the paper cast in the sun to dry. This could take 1 to 3 days. When you peel the dry paper from the objects, it will be embossed with your collage.

Other Uses ∾

Handmade paper is a great surface for watercolor painting. And you can stamp or print on the handmade paper, too (see pages 112–115 for techniques).

Miniature Glass Suncatcher

Tiny bits of pressed plant material sandwiched between panes of glass make up this elegant project. Save interestingly shaped and colored leaves and petals; use your sense of design to combine them into one-of-a-kind glass keepsakes. Hang them in windows, tie them to the ribbon on a wrapped gift package, or use them to decorate your Christmas tree.

MATERIALS

Tiny leaves and blossoms
2 glass microscope slides
1 egg white
Clear glue (Durabond or other brands recommended for glass)
Straight pin or toothpick, for applying glue
⅛″ wide satin or grosgrain ribbon, about 16″ long

1 Save the tiny blossoms from a variety of herbs and flowers in your garden. Thyme, sage, lavender, marjoram, chives, rue, bee balm, and hyssop all have tiny florets, and the smaller leaves of bay and costmary can be used. Press these items in a flower press (page 6) or between layers of paper towels in the pages of a heavy phone book.

2 Arrange the plant material carefully on one of the glass slides, securing with egg white beaten until slightly foamy, applied with the point of a pin or toothpick. You can use glue for this, but egg white will dry invisible.

3 When the composition is complete and the egg white or glue is dry, cover with the second slide and secure the corners with a tiny drop of glue (use glue, not egg white, for this and the remaining parts of the project). Press securely until dry.

4 With the ribbon, make a 1″ loop, leaving 4″–5″ of ribbon at one end. Glue the loop to the top center of the glass, spreading the longer length of ribbon so that half its width laps over the front of the glass and half laps over the back, forming a frame.

5 Once the loop has dried in place, glue the longer length of ribbon all the way around the glass, covering the raw edges on front and back and ending at the top center.

6 Use the two 4″–5″ lengths of ribbon to tie a bow around the glued loop, and trim the ends.

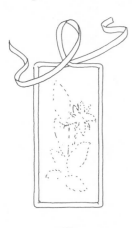

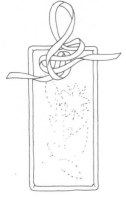

Decorating a Glasstop Table ∾

Here is a beautiful way to decorate a glasstop table. Spread a white or pastel tablecloth on the table, under the glass. Randomly scatter dried flower petals onto the tablecloth. Replace the glass. The petals make a lovely display, temporary though it is, and you can still clean the glass without disturbing the design.

Pressing Flowers ∾

You can also quick-press some flowers using the method thaught to 19th-century botany students. It not only dries the plant, but coats it with a thin film of wax as well. Sandwich the plant material between sheets of waxed paper, cover with a press cloth or sheet of kraft paper, and iron on the synthetic setting until the plant is dry. Some flowers will lose their color over time, particularly if they are exposed to bright light. You may dye them with water-based paints or inks before waxing them.

CHAPTER 4

Gifts from the Sewing Basket

*A*ll the gifts in this chapter require the use of needle and thread. A sewing machine is also recommended. The projects combine sewing, decorating, and blending scents to create a variety of useful and pleasurable gifts. Both needlework and the knowledge of and use of herbs are traditional women's work. It is a tremendous boost to remember this — history shows that women have healed and clothed civilization; we have dealt in basic human needs and comforts. If you like to sew, I think you'll enjoy making these projects for yourself and your loved ones.

Scented Draft Dodger

A draft dodger is a densely filled fabric tube that, when placed along the bottom edge of a drafty door, will help prevent drafts from coming through. Here we are taking advantage of the draft itself; the gentle air flow that manages to pass through the fabric barricade carries the aroma of the scented filling into the room.

MATERIALS

- ½ yard lining fabric, tightly woven cotton sheeting or twill
- ½ yard cover fabric, bottom-weight twill or upholstery
- ½ yard ½" elastic
- 4–5 cups all-clay cat litter
- 4–5 cups cedar shavings
- 1 dram (60 drops) essential oils, scent or blend of your choice

EQUIPMENT

Needle and thread or sewing machine
Large bowl or bucket

1 Cut the inner lining pieces according to the cutting diagram: two 4½" circles and one rectangle, 11" x 37", and the cover fabric 12" x 40". If you want to decorate the cover fab-

ric, do so before sewing it (see pages 109–15 for techniques). The only parts of the fabric that will be concealed in seams are 1½" at either end and ½" along the long edges.

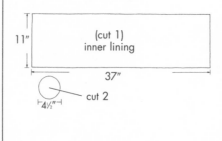

11" — (cut 1) inner lining — 37"
cut 2 — 4½"

12" — (cut 1) cover fabric area to be decorated — 40"

2 To make the inner bag: Turn under and press ½" toward the wrong side of the fabric, on one end of the rectangle. Turn under and press ½" around the circumference of one of the circles.

3 Stitch the other end of the rectangle to the unpressed circle, using a ½" seam allowance and keeping right sides facing.

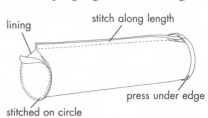

lining — stitch along length
press under edge
stitched on circle

4 Stitch down the length of the rectangle. Turn the lining right-side out.

MAKING THE FILLING

5 In large bowl or bucket, mix cat litter with cedar shavings. Drop 1 dram (60 drops) of essential oils onto mixture, stirring to disperse the oils. The oil mixture can be one scent or a blend. Citrus and mint are refreshing; florals like lavender and rose are fragrant and relaxing; sandalwood, frankincense, and myrrh have an earthy scent; combine the cedar with rosemary, cinnamon, or clove for the holidays. Pour filling into lining, using a canning funnel to direct filling into the opening.

6 Carefully pin the second circle to the filled tube, wrong sides together, and hand stitch them together using small, close stitches.

Note: Filling the bag from one end is easiest, but hand stitching the circle can be tricky. If you prefer, you can machine stitch the circles onto both ends of the tube and leave the filling opening at the center of the seam that runs the length of the tube. As you fill, stuff it down to both ends of the tube and then hand stitch the seam closed.

MAKING THE OUTER COVER

7 On both short ends of the cover rectangle, turn and press under ½" and then 1" to make an elastic casing. Stitch at ⅞" (⅛" in from the inner edge), and again at ⅛" in from the outer edge.

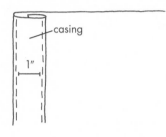

8 Cut two pieces of elastic so that when they are fully extended, they stretch to 12". Attach a safety pin to one end of elastic and feed it into one of the casings. Stitch the other end of the elastic to the casing end, ¼" in from the edge. Now, pull the safety pin and elastic through to the other end of the casing (it will gather the fabric with it). Making sure that it is not twisted, pin the elastic to the end of the casing, remove the safety pin, and stitch the elastic to the casing ¼" in from the edge. Repeat for the casing at the other end of the cover.

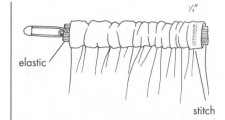

9 Pin right sides together and then stitch the long seam of the cover. Maintain a ½" seam allowance, catching the elastic casings at each end.

10 Slip the elastic tube over the filled inner bag, and find a drafty door for your draft dodger!

Refreshing the Scent ❧

The scented inner bag should last quite a long time. If you find that the scent has faded, however, remove the cover and drop more essential oil onto the fabric liner. If you tire of the original scent, open the liner, replace the filling with a new batch, and stitch it back together.
Note: The outer cover can be removed and laundered as needed.

Herb-Stamped Pillow

This pillow — covered in fabric you have decorated in an herbal motif — makes a lovely gift. These instructions are for a pillow filled with plain fiberfill batting, but I encourage you to add a handful or a pillowful of fragrant herbs to the pillow stuffing. (See pages 112–113 for stamping techniques.) Lemony herbs, florals (lavender, rose, chamomile), or exotics (sandalwood, frankincense) are lovely choices.

MATERIALS

White or pastel-colored fabric,
  16" x 32"
Fabric paints
1 fine black permanent marker, or
  tube of squeezable fine-line fabric
  paint
Sponges or foam rubber
Fiberfill batting, enough to stuff a
  15" square pillow

EQUIPMENT

Scissors
Paintbrushes
Containers for paint mixing and
  stamping
Iron or machine dryer
Needle and thread or sewing
  machine

1 Launder the fabric to remove any sizing. This will enable the paints to penetrate. Cut two 16" x 16" squares.

2 Cut leaf and flower shapes out of the sponge or foam, and use them to stamp the fabric. For more detail, use the brushes and fine-line markers/paints to add leaf veins, flower stamens, etc. after the stamped paint has dried.

details

3 Allow the paint to dry fully. "Set" your designs into the fabric with an iron or machine dryer, as instructed on the paint container.

4 Pin the two squares together, right sides facing each other, and stitch, using a ½" seam allowance, around all four corners. Leave an opening of 6"–8" along one side for the stuffing. Clip the corners.

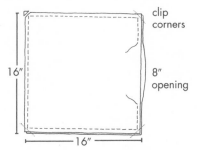

clip corners

16"

8" opening

16"

5 Turn the pillow right-side out. Iron the seams flat, carefully pressing in the seam allowances at the opening, which you will later hand sew. (If you want to add tassels, refer to the directions below and attach them at the corners now.)

6 Fill the pillow with batting and herbs, if desired, distributing it as evenly as possible. By hand, sew the opening with small slip stitches or a blind stitch.

Simple Tassels for Your Pillow Corners

MATERIALS
Piece of cardboard about 5″ x 5″
Yarn, twine, metallic thread, or other interesting string

1 Wrap the yarn carefully around the cardboard, in parallel rows, until you have a nice handful of yarn.

2 Carefully cut the yarn at both ends of the board, keeping the pieces lined up straight.

3 With a piece of yarn about 10″ long, tie around the bundle of yarn, right in the middle.

4 Fold the bundle in half and carefully wrap yarn around it, leaving a "bulb" at the top and lining up the ends of the yarn at the bottom as best you can.

5 Wrap the center of the tassel, and knot the wrapping yarn and trim it or incorporate it into the hanging tassel yarn. If you want a more decorative wrap, thread a needle with yarn and overcast the wrapping yarns in the other direction.

overcast stiches

6 Trim the bottom of the tassel.

7 To attach the tassel to your pillow, using yarn and a yarn needle or sewing thread on a regular needle, push the needle out from each inside corner of the pillow and catch the tassel tie. Stitch in and out several times, catching the tie each time. Anchor and knot the thread or yarn to the inside of the pillow.

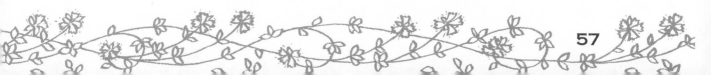

Sachets

Once you begin to create sachets, you'll probably find them irresistible. You'll need to purchase a few ingredients, such as the fixative and the oils, but the rest can be grown in your garden. The sachet bags can be made from scrap material and kept ready to use whenever the spirit moves you to make a batch of potpourri.

MATERIALS

For each bag, finished size 4" x 2½"

6" x 6" piece of tightly woven fabric (cotton or silk is classic)
Sewing thread
Ribbon
Rubber band (optional)

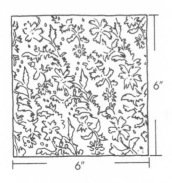

6"

6"

1 Turn under (toward wrong side) and press ½", then 1" of fabric on one edge, and stitch ⅛" in from the bottom of the hem (or ⅞" down from top edge of hem).

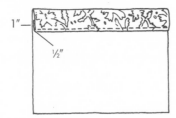

1"

½"

2 With right sides facing, fold the bag in half and stitch ½" from edge on the two raw edges.

3 Clip the raw-edged corner and turn the bag right-side out. Press seams.

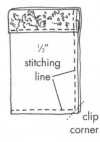

½"
stitching
line

clip
corner

FILLING THE SACHETS

4 If your fabric is not tightly woven, make inner bags, following the instructions for the inner bathbag pouches on page 26, but make the bags 2" x 2½".

5 Fill the sachet bags (or inner bags) about ⅔ full with sachet mix, about 3 tablespoons.

6 Tie a ribbon around the bag, around the seam line from the hem. If the ribbon is not secure enough, fasten the bag closed with a rubber band first, then hide the rubber band with the ribbon.

Sachet Fillings

Keep these fillings in a glass jar with an airtight lid and age them for several weeks before using. This allows the oils and fixative to blend, and for all the scents to meld. These recipes make large batches — enough to fill several dozen sachets. You can store any extra filling in the jar for later use.

Note: Also see Potpourris on page 108 for more recipes.

Forever Lavender Sachet

16	ounces lavender flowers
2	ounces sweet woodruff
½	ounce oak moss
½	ounce thyme
8	ounces dried orange peel
4	ounces gum benzoin
	Several handfuls of other herbs and flowers (such as peppermint, violets, rose geranium petals)
¼	ounce cloves and anise, combined

Combine all of the ingredients and shake occasionally during aging.

Very Lemon Sachet

1	pound dried lemon peel
1	pound cut orrisroot
⅛	ounce oil of lemongrass
½	ounce oil of lemon peel
1	ounce oil of bergamot

Put the lemon peel in the jar. Add the orrisroot. Add the oils and allow them to seep down into the mix, shaking occasionally.

Making Polymer Clay Charms ∾

Hang a homemade charm that signals the scent of the sachet from the ribbon of the sachet bag. Use polymer clay, and make the charm around a piece of wire or a jewelry eye pin, so you'll have a loop to thread the ribbon through. Model a sprig of lavender, using a sage green stem formed around wire, with little lavender-colored florets on the stem. Make a lemon slice with bright yellow peel, white pulp, and a mixture of white and yellow for the citrus sections. Push an eye pin through the length of each finished piece and oven-cure your designs according to the manufacturer's directions.

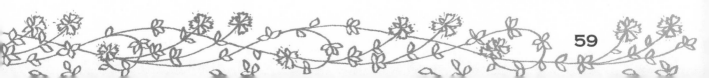

Painted Canvas Floorcloth

Canvas floorcloths used as decoration are making a comeback. It's really not unusual to be painting on canvas — artists have been doing it for centuries! These floorcloths are finished with a clear varnish to protect the artwork, and I suggest several ways to complete them so that they have a finished, professional look.

MATERIALS

Heavy canvas, at least 12 ounce,
   24″ x 36″
Acrylic primer or gesso
Acrylic paints
Clear varnish, water based
Rug binding, 3 yards of 1″ wide
Liquid rubber or rubber rug liner
   and foam padding (optional)

EQUIPMENT

Variety of brushes, including one 3″
   flat (for priming and varnishing)
Heavy needle and carpet thread

1 Draw a ½″ border around the perimeter of the canvas. (This will be turned under later to finish the cloth edges.)

2 Paint primer on one side of the cloth, painting up to the pencil line you have just drawn. If you don't plan to line the bottom of the cloth, prime that side of the cloth too. Paint a second coat of primer on the front of the cloth.

3 Using acrylic paints, decorate the floorcloth as you please. If you prefer to stencil, stamp, or print, see pages 110–115 for techniques. Create your own herbal design adapted from old botanical illustrations, or letter your favorite herb-related quotation.

4 When the paint is completely dry, apply two coats of varnish with the 3″ flat brush, being careful not to "scrub" with the brush, as varnishes can foam and become cloudy. Use smooth, steady strokes across the entire piece. Allow the varnish to dry between coats. If you don't intend to finish the bottom, as described in the next section, paint it with two coats of varnish as well.

FINISHING THE FLOORCLOTH

Fringing: The simplest finish is to fringe the four edges up to the border. If you have a sewing machine, stitch along the border line to prevent further threads from raveling; then pull the outer yarns to create the fringe. If you don't have a sewing machine, hand stitch a tiny running stitch around the edge to hold threads in place.

Binding: Stitch 1″ rug binding around the edge of the cloth along the ½″ line, with the binding facing the painted surface. Trim the border of the floorcloth to ¼″. Now turn the binding under along the seam line and press around the entire piece. By hand, sew the binding to the underside of the cloth, using small stitches that don't penetrate to the face of the cloth.

Rubberizing the underside: "Liquid rubber" is a new product that is painted on the underside of the cloth to create a nonskid rubbery surface. Do not paint the rug binding.

Padding and rubberizing the floorcloth: Follow the instructions for binding the edge of the piece, but before you stitch the binding to the underside, enclose a layer of batting or foam rubber or a piece of an old mattress cover, and then a sheet of nonskid carpet liner (rubber webbing). Hand stitch the binding onto the last layer, keeping everything as flat as possible. In order to prevent all of these lay-

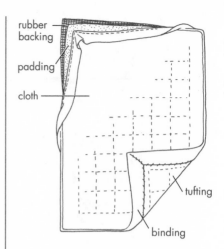

ers from shifting, stitch through the entire sandwich, either as a border 1″ in from the finished edge or in a decorative way, such as tufting every 4 inches. (Tufting consists of stitching through all of the layers to create a thick-and-thin effect, similar to quilting.)

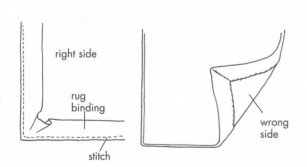

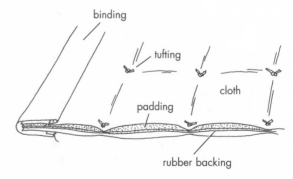

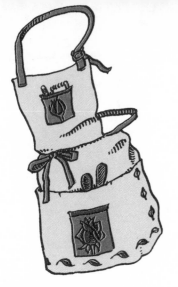

Harvest Apron

This apron — at home in both garden and kitchen — makes an attractive gift. The chest pocket is sized for herb seed packets and a marking pen, the lower pockets can hold tools, and the neck and waist straps are adjustable. Decorate the apron with an herb motif to personalize it as a gift for your favorite gardener or cook.

MATERIALS

1 yard cotton canvas or twill fabric, prewashed

Needle and thread or sewing machine

4 yards double-folded seam binding

3 yards 1″ cotton webbing or heavy twill tape (for straps)

Two 1″ metal D-rings

1 Mark the pattern pieces on the fabric:

One 18″ x 18″ square for the apron bottom (with rounded bottom corners) connected to the apron bib, 8″ across the top, 18″ at the bottom, 12″ high

Two 6″ x 6″ pockets

One 8″ x 18″ tool pocket (with rounded bottom corners)

Note: You can decorate the fabric pieces before or after marking and cutting, or after the

Cutting diagram

apron is assembled. Use fabric paints, or see pages 109–115 for other techniques.

2 Cut out the pieces.

3 Attach the seam binding to the top edges of the three pocket pieces by sandwiching the fabric between the binding and stitching, catching both sides of the binding. *Note:* One side of the binding extends slightly farther out than the other. Place the extended side behind the fabric as you sew, which helps ensure that you catch it in the seam.

4 Turn under ½″ and press the side edges of the two 6″ pockets.

5 **Chest pocket:** Pin one pocket so that it is 8″ down from the top edge of the bib, upside down, with right sides together. Stitch, backstitching at both ends of the seam. Flip the pocket up and sew sides to the bib, ⅛″ in from the pocket edges, backstitching several times at the pocket corners. Stitch a seam 2″ in from one edge; this makes the slot for holding pens.

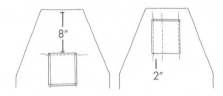

6 **Lower pockets:** Pin the bottom edge of the other 6″ pocket in the center of the larger lower pocket, 1″ up from the bottom edge, upside down, with right sides together. Stitch, backstitching at both ends of the

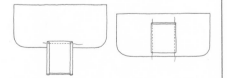

seam. Flip the pocket up and stitch sides to the larger pocket, ⅛″ in from the pocket edges, backstitching at the pocket corners several times.

7 Pin the large pocket to the apron bottom, right side of the apron facing the wrong side of the pocket. Stitch lines 6″ in from each outer edge to form the center 6″ pocket. Stitch around the outer edge of the large pocket, using a ¼″ seam allowance.

8 Use seam binding to bind around the entire apron body, catching the raw edges of the pocket as you sew around the lower half. Start and end the binding at an upper bib corner or on the bib bottom, so the binding join will be concealed underneath the straps.

9 Cut three 20″ lengths of webbing or tape for strap, and one 3″ length. Fold under 1″ on the 20″ lengths and stitch one to each side of the waist, just where the bib ends on the front of the apron. Use a box stitch to hold the strap on securely. Sew the other 20″ length to the left

top corner of the bib, on the front, using a box stitch.

10 Fold under 1″ of the 3″ length of strapping and pin it to the right-hand corner of the bib. Thread the D-rings through the remaining 1″, and tuck the end under the 1″ fold so that it will be caught in the back of the box stitch. Box stitch through all three layers of strapping to secure the D-rings to the apron.

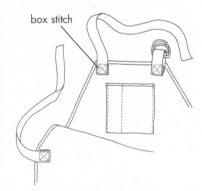

box stitch

11 Thread the longer length of neck strap through both D-rings and then back out through only one D-ring to hold it in place. Adjust the strap to fit your neck. If you did not decorate the pockets before you began sewing, do so now!

Scented Hot Pads

This quilted hot pad is actually a fabric envelope that holds a scented mixture. When placed under a hot teapot or casserole, the pad gives off a spicy aroma while protecting the tabletop from the heat. The inner pouch can be freshened to rejuvenate the scent; the outer envelope is washable.

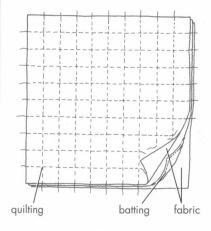

1 Sandwich the cotton batting between two layers of cotton fabric. Stitch quilting lines every 1″ in both directions.

quilting   batting   fabric

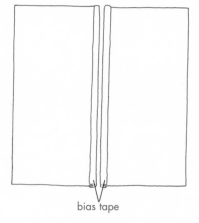

2 Cut the third piece of cotton fabric in half. Stitch bias tape along a 10″ edge of each piece.

bias tape

MATERIALS

Three 10″ x 10″ pieces of cotton fabric
10″ x 10″ piece of cotton batting
2 yards seam bias tape, double folded, ½″ or wider
Two 9″ x 9″ pieces of cotton muslin or sheeting

EQUIPMENT

Needle and thread or sewing machine

3 With wrong sides facing, lay the two bias-taped (back) pieces on top of the quilted (front) piece, butting the taped edges against each other in the center of the pad.

4 Stitch the bias tape around the four sides of the hot pad, turning under the edge at the end of the tape to form a clean finish. *Note:* The folded bias tape has one side that extends out farther than the other. Place the extended side under the fabric, to ensure that you will catch the binding in the back.

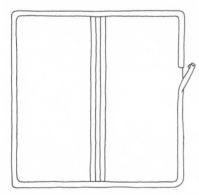

5 To make the inner pouch, stitch the muslin squares together around all four corners, leaving a 3″–4″ opening along one edge. Turn right-side out and press.

MAKING THE FILLING

Use these ingredients individually or in any combination:

Whole cloves
Whole allspice
Dried citrus peel
Broken cinnamon sticks
Star anise
Rosemary

Make about ½ cup of spicy mixture and place it in the pouch. Stitch the pouch closed. Slip the pouch into the quilted pad and flatten the contents as much as possible.

Filling Options ↝

↝ If you prefer a different scent for your filling, you can fill the pouch with cut orrisroot or cellulosic fiber fixative (see page 108) that has been aged for several weeks with the essential oil of your choice. For ½ cup of fixative, use 10–15 drops of oil to start, and adjust to your taste.

↝ Make the pads half the size and use them as coasters for hot drinks.

↝ Decorate the face panel of the pad before quilting it. Then, instead of quilting in straight lines, quilt around the shapes of your design.

↝ For the holidays, make a long table runner filled with spices. When you serve the hot dishes for that special dinner, placing them along the runner will release a festive aroma.

↝ A scented hot pad would make a great addition to a gift basket. Combined with homemade teas, flavored honey, and a unique cup or mug, you'll have a gift that tastes and smells wonderful, and will leave the recipient feeling loved.

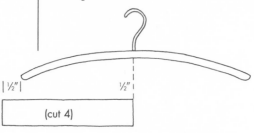

Moth-Repellent Hangers

Many herbs have a natural capacity to repel insects. Use them with sweeter smelling herbs to create hangers that will keep your fine woolens safe from moths. The moth-repellent herb mix can also be used in small sachet bags; hang them in closets or place in drawers full of sweaters.

MATERIALS

For 1 padded hanger

2 yards satin blanket binding, about 2″ wide if ironed flat, or 2″ satin ribbon, or satin fabric cut into 2″ strips

Wooden hanger

12″ ribbon, about ½″ wide

White glue

Filling (see next section for details)

EQUIPMENT

Iron

Yardstick or measuring tape

Needle and thread or sewing machine

1 If you are using blanket binding, press open the folds along both edges to get a flat ribbon.

2 Measure the wooden hanger from the center to one end. Cut four pieces of the wide satin 1″ longer than this measurement. Press under ½″ along one end of each piece.

| ½″ | | ½″ |
| (cut 4) | | |

3 Stitch the strips into two tubes, open at the pressed end, using a ½″ seam allowance. For rounded ends, stitch the end of the tube in a curved shape.

4 Turn the tubes right-side out and press them flat.

5 Slip the tubes onto the hanger and pack them with herbal filling. Use tiny stitches or blindstitch to sew up the center seam.

6 Wrap the hanger hook with the narrow ribbon and glue it in place. Now, wrap the ribbon around the hanger, placing it over the hand-sewn seam. Stitch it in place. Tie a bow at the base of the hanger hook.

Filling the Hanger

Follow this recipe (from Heritage Farms in Richmond, N.H.) exactly as it is or make your own blend with at least two of the repellents (R) and one of the oils (O) listed.

INGREDIENTS

½   cup cedar shavings (R)
¼   cup pennyroyal (R)
¼   cup lavender (R)
¼   cup santolina or southernwood (R)
¼   cup peppermint (R)
¼   cup lemon verbena
¼   cup thyme
¼   cup rosemary
¼   cup orrisroot
⅛   cup whole cloves
⅛   cup dried lemon peel
⅛   cup black peppercorns
6   drops each of cedar, lemon, and lavender oils (O)
3   drops each of pennyroyal*, peppermint, and bayberry oils (O)

Mix ingredients together, drop the oils on top, and allow to age, shaking occasionally, for at least 3 weeks, before filling hangers and sachets.

Moth-Repellent Fillings

Start with a base of two or more of the following moth-repellent herbs:

santolina
southernwood (or other artemesias including wormwood)
pennyroyal*
pyrethrum (the yellow flower centers only)
tansy

Add one of the following pleasant-smelling herbs:

red cedar
camphor basil (Mint family)
lavender

Many of the most powerful plants listed above smell awful. Therefore, most herbal moth repellents are blended with sweeter-smelling herbs and flowers to improve the aroma.

Do not forget to use a fixative — such as orrisroot chips or cellulosic fiber — if you want your hanger's power to last.

*Note: Pregnant women should avoid all contact with pennyroyal.

Garden-Printed Tote Bag

The pattern for this tote bag allows you to print one piece of fabric and stitch it together without cutting up your design. The finished bag is approximately the size of a grocery bag. Two inner pockets offer secure storage, and the handles extend under the bag to support heavy loads. See pages 113 – 115 for more information about nature printing.

MATERIALS

1¼ yards of bottom-weight cotton twill or canvas, at least 45″ width
Fabric paints with extender
Herbs for nature printing
3 yards cotton webbing (sold for belts)

EQUIPMENT

Chalk or pencil
Yardstick or ruler
Scissors
Plastic plates or palette for mixing and stamping paints
Paintbrushes and/or dabber
Sewing machine

1 Launder the fabric to remove the sizing so that the fabric paints can penetrate.

2 Iron the fabric, if necessary. Using chalk or a pencil, measure and mark the pattern pieces on the fabric. The dotted lines represent the ½″ seam allowance and 2″ hems, which will be hidden after the sewing is complete. Decorate within the dotted lines.

3 Print the fabric, using mint leaves and flowers, lavender spikes, lamb's ears leaves, or leaves like lady's mantle or burnet. Add detail with a paintbrush. Cure the fabric with an iron or in the dryer, following the paint manufacturer's directions.

4 Cut out the pattern pieces.

5 **Pockets:** Turn and press under ¾″ twice on the top edge of the pockets. Stitch ⅝″ down from the top. Stitch again ⅛″ from the top. Press under ½″ on the remaining three sides of the pockets. Pin the pockets onto the wrong side of the larger bag panels, locating the top edge of the pocket 5″ down from the raw edge of the bag. Using a neutral color thread, stitch the sides and bottom of the pockets, ⅛″ in from the edge, leaving the top hemmed edge open. (The thread will show on the outside — the strapping will cover the side seams, but not the bottom seam of the pockets.) Backstitch several times at the pocket corners.

Cutting diagram

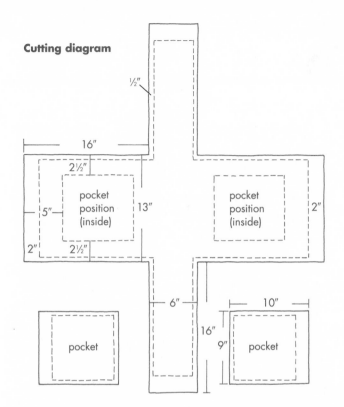

16″

2½″

pocket position (inside)

5″

13″

pocket position (inside)

2″

2″

2½″

6″

16″

9″

10″

pocket

pocket

½″

Stitching diagram

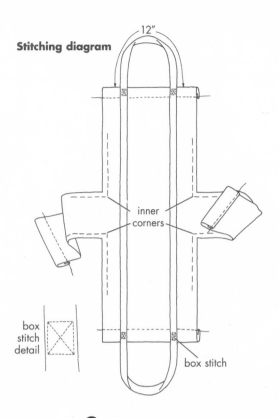

12″

inner corners

box stitch detail

box stitch

6 Turn and press under 1″ twice on each hem edge of the tote bag. Stitch ⅞″ in from the edge, and again ⅛″ in from the edge.

7 **Strap handles:** Measure in 2½″ from both raw edges of the larger bag panels and draw guidelines for the straps, on the right side of the fabric, down the full length of the bag. Starting at the bag bottom, pin the strap toward the inside of the guideline, leaving a 12″ loop at the ends for the handles. Don't let the loop twist as you turn. Stitch along both sides, ⅛″ in from the edges. At the end of the strap, turn under 1″, cover the raw edge where the strap began, and sew a box stitch. For extra security at the strap handles, sew box stitches at the four points where the strap leaves the fabric.

8 Starting at each inner corner, with right sides facing, pin and then stitch, using a ½″ seam allowance, up to the bag opening, taking care to ensure that the upper hems line up. Stitch each seam twice; backstitch at the upper corners. Turn the bag right-side out.

CHAPTER 5

Gifts for the Gardener

Gardening gifts are always welcome. As a gardener myself, I know that there is always more to learn, new seed varieties to try, new tools and decorative items to make and use. A gift for the garden recognizes this, and says "I know this is a precious part of your life, and I want to support your effort."

Gardening makes some feel that they must have a "green thumb"; many are intimidated. Presenting a new gardener with gifts for the garden offers encouragement and provides an incentive to keep trying, to keep learning, and to enjoy the process. Whether you give a new gardener a basket of seed and soil mix or a seasoned gardener a file box for her many seed packets, these gifts are sure to please.

The day will come when a single carrot,

freshly observed ... will set off a revolution.

— Paul Cézanne

Painted Watering Can

A painted watering bucket filled with dried flowers from your summer garden makes a lovely display. Use one outdoors during the season; then bring it indoors during the cooler months to remind you of your garden. Whether your intention is to make a practical gift or an ornamental one, use plants and books for reference.

MATERIALS

Galvanized metal watering can
Vinegar and a clean rag
Acrylic paints and gloss medium, or
Oil-based enamels with thinner

EQUIPMENT

Masking tape
Carbon paper, to trace a design
Pencil
Various brushes — round, oval, flat,
  thick, thin

1 Remove the oily finish from the metal by wiping it with the clean rag and a solution of 3 parts water to 1 part vinegar.

2 *Optional*: Paint background before transferring your design to the can.

3 If you have drawn or traced a design, tape it to the container and slip a piece of carbon paper underneath. Use the pencil to transfer the outline onto the metal.

4 Paint the basic leaf and flower shapes in the dominant color, using a relatively large brush. To blend colors, do so while the first coat is wet.

5 Add details like veins and flower parts when first layer is dry, using a fine brush.

6 When the painting is complete and dry, brush acrylic medium or varnish over the design, or use acrylic spray finish.

lady's mantle

sorrel

borage

basil

Decoupaged Seed File Box

Anyone who gardens from seed knows how important it is to keep seeds organized. I keep a box, sorted by plant type, that is invaluable all spring, summer, and fall, and it serves as a storage file in winter.

This box, designed to fit standard-sized seed packets, is decorated with herb motifs from catalogs and saved seed packets.

MATERIALS

Stiff cardboard, mat board,
  or illustration board, 18″ x 24″
Masking tape
Seed packets, pictures of herbs from
  catalogs or gardening magazines
Decoupage medium (Mod-Podge,
  acrylic medium, or thinned white
  glue)
1 yard grosgrain ribbon, 1″ wide
6″ length of carpet thread or yarn
4″ x 6″ piece of felt for bottom
  (optional)
1 paper fastener

EQUIPMENT

Cutting surface, such as cork, wood
  or rubber
X-acto or mat knife, sharp blades
Metal ruler, 18″ if available
Scissors
1″ flat brush

1 In pencil, draw the pattern for the box and lid onto the board. The dotted lines are fold lines; the solid lines are cutting lines.

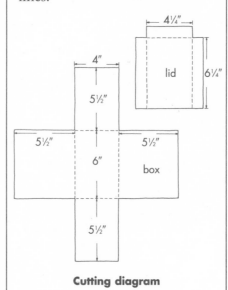

Cutting diagram

2 Using the metal ruler and sharp knife, cut out the shapes. Score lightly along the dotted lines, cutting only halfway through the board, to allow you to fold these lines.

3 Fold along the scored lines and run masking tape along each seam line to fasten the corners. The upper edges of the box, if cut accurately, should line up perfectly. If they don't, trim them before you tape the box together.

4 Cut out images from the seed packets and catalogs.

5 To decoupage the box and lid, coat an area of the board with acrylic medium or glue, stick on the paper cutout, and brush over it to hold it in place and seal it. Decorate around the upper edges of the box and down at least 1″ inside the box.

6 The box lid edges will be trimmed with the grosgrain ribbon. You can decoupage the top only, or the entire lid, both inside and out.

7 When your design is complete, paint a final coat of acrylic medium onto the box and lid. If you have been using white glue for the decoupage, use acrylic gloss medium for the final coat (glue may leave a cloudy film).

8 Paint a 1″ stripe of glue or medium around the lid front and side edges and along the top of the lid back. Cut three 3″ lengths of ribbon for the hinges. Glue the grosgrain ribbon hinges onto the lid back, ¼″ in from each edge and ¼″ apart. Glue the yarn or carpet thread to the center front of the lid. Glue the rest of the ribbon around the entire lid edge, covering the hinge and yarn ends.

9 To finish the ribbon hinges, glue the three ribbon ends to the inside of the box, spaced ½″ from each edge and from each other.

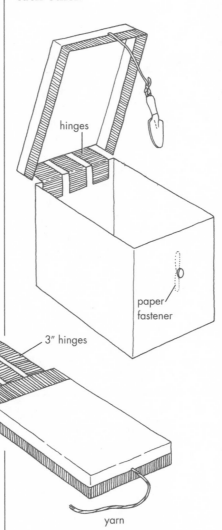

hinges

paper fastener

3″ hinges

hinges

yarn

10 Measure 3″ down the front of the box. Pierce a hole in the box and insert the paper fastener. Wrapping the yarn or carpet thread around this "button" fastens the file box closed.

11 Glue the felt to the bottom of the box.

12 If you want to include index dividers for the file box, mark them on the leftover board and cut them with the sharp knife. Leave them blank, or make indexes for the different types of herbs, such as Edible, Aromatic, Medicinal, Mints, Culinary, Insect Repellent, and Healing.

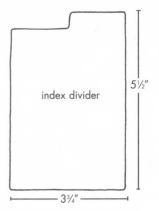

index divider

5½″

3¾″

Plant Markers

If you're like me, showing off your garden is one of the joys of the season. People like to know what's growing, especially when they don't recognize the plants by sight. Markers are a decorative way to remind yourself what seeds are planted where, and to inform visitors about what they're looking at.

MATERIALS

3″ x 4″ pieces of hardboard, ¼″ thick
Medium-grit sandpaper
Primer
Acrylic paints
Small brushes
1″ flat brush
Varnish (oil-based exterior type)
Wooden stakes made from ¾″ x 1½″
  stock (called 1 x 2)
1½″ galvanized nails

EQUIPMENT

Drill with bit large enough to make
  a hole to fit over nail heads
Hand saw

1 Cut the 3″ x 4″ rectangles with a saw, or have them cut to size at the hardware or lumber store. One 2″ x 4″ sheet of hardboard will yield 96 rectangles. Sand the edges, using medium-grit sandpaper.

2 Drill a hole in each piece of wood, centered, ½″ down from one of the 3″ ends. Sand the surface of the board if necessary.

3 Coat both sides and all edges of each piece of board with primer and allow it to dry.

4 For a set of coordinated markers, choose a border color and paint a stripe of acrylic paint in that color around all of the pieces. You can also paint the backs in that color.

5 Using seed packets as your reference, paint the name of the plant and a sprig of its foliage onto the board.

6 Allow the paint to dry thoroughly.

7 Using the flat brush, paint several coats of varnish over both sides of the wood and in the drilled hole, allowing each coat to dry before applying the next.

8 Taper the stakes at the bottom by sawing a diagonal at one end. (Or you can purchase wire stakes at a gardening store or pretapered wooden stakes at a lumberyard.)

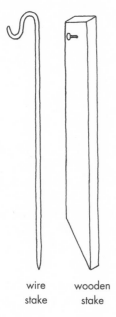

wire stake   wooden stake

9 Pound a nail into each wooden stake, leaving ¾″ exposed to hang the marker on.

Polymer Clay Plant Markers

MATERIALS
Makes 8 markers
1 pound white polymer clay
Several 2-ounce packages of other colors, particularly green
Water-based varnish
1″ flat brush

EQUIPMENT
Rolling pin
Glass casserole dish or cookie sheet

1 Prepare the white clay according to instructions on the package. Roll out large sections of the clay ³⁄₁₆″ thick, and cut out 3″ x 4″ rectangles. Make a hole through each rectangle at least ½″ down from the top, centered along one of the 3″ edges and large enough to fit over the nail heads. Bake these blanks in the oven according to the manufacturer's directions.

2 Using the colored clays, make leaf and flower shapes that look like the plants you will be marking. Roll small cylindrical lengths and spell out the plant name. Make these as decorative as you like. They could be somewhat three-dimensional, with bits of clay foliage jutting out from the surface. Be sure to anchor each piece of the design firmly onto the baked blanks.

3 Bake again according to the instructions.

4 Coat both sides of the markers with water-based varnish.

5 Hang from wooden or wire stakes in the garden.

Variation: Using polymer clay with a stiff wire baked directly into it, you can make small markers with the names of your houseplants on them. If you give a plant as a gift, remove the paper tag that comes with it and make a clay marker with a personal touch instead.

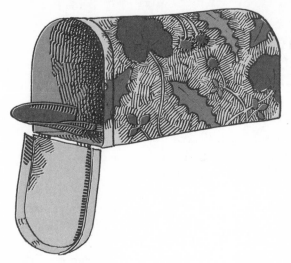

Stenciled Tool Storage Mailbox

We gardeners often leave our tools out in the rain, and then experience frustration when the tool turns up rusty. A storage unit in the garden is a great way to solve this problem, and it will add a decorative touch to the garden at the same time. See page 111 for stenciling techniques.

MATERIALS

Metal mailbox

Newspaper

Indoor/outdoor satin finish enamel spray paint, one light, one dark color

Openwork lace or paper doilies (optional)

Stencils, store-bought or homemade

Spray adhesive (the type that allows for repositioning)

Stencil brushes, ¼" and ½"

Acrylic paint with gloss medium and/or stencil creme paints

Small liner brush

Spray polyurethane (varnish)

1 Working in a well-ventilated area with newspaper protecting the surfaces beneath and behind the mailbox, spray paint the out-side of the box with the white or pastel color. Work in very thin coats, allowing the paint to dry between applications.

2 Cut your stencils. Make your own stencils using simple herb motifs like lady's mantle, fern fronds, and sorrel leaves for larger shapes, and lavender florets, chamomile flowers, and thyme sprigs for daintier stencils. You can stencil a picket fence all around the box, with an assortment of herbs and flowers in front of or behind the fence. Or make tiny stencils of a variety of herbs and scatter them all over the box.

3 Position one or more stencils on the box, using the spray adhesive or masking tape. Mix the acrylic paints with some medium, or, if you are using creme paints, select the colors you want to use. Dip the stencil brush into the paint and wipe the brush in a circular motion on paper toweling until it appears almost dry. This works paint up into the bristles and removes excess paint from the tips. (Too much paint on the brush will cause it to seep under the stencil.) To apply the paint, use a counterclockwise, circular motion, starting at the edge of the stencil and working toward the center. Or you can use a stipple technique — bounce the brush up and down, working from the edges toward the center. You will be building up

color in layers. Allow the paint to dry slightly, then repeat the process. Apply shading or highlights with other colors within the stencil as you work.

4 Remove stencil when finished painting, and allow the paints to cure for at least 48 hours.

5 Apply a coat of polyurethane spray to the entire box, using the method described in step 1.

6 Mount the finished box on a stake in a convenient place in your garden, and keep important tools in it.

Variation: You can paint the mailbox one color, or mask off large shapes with tape to create stripes or blotches of colors. For a romantic, Victorian look, drape a sheet of openwork lace over the mailbox, or affix several paper doilies with temporary adhesive. Use a light color so that your stencil colors will cover this layer. If there are areas where you don't want this pattern, cover them with newspaper. Spray over the openwork, being careful not to move it. Allow the paint to dry before removing the lace or other masking materials.

Garden Hand Tools Make Great Gifts ∾

Any or all of these tools would fit easily in the Tool Storage Mailbox!

Hand trowel: Small shovel used for planting bulbs, transplanting small starts, and weeding. A straight-shank trowel is helpful for bulb planting. A drop-shank trowel is good for general use.

Cultivators and hoes: These are for close work on your hands and knees. The tool end is shaped like a full-sized tool (fork, hoe), but smaller, and has a short handle.

Pruning shears: Anvil shears and hook-and-blade shears are essential tools for pruning.

Hori-Hori knife: A Japanese gardening tool, shaped like a long, slightly concave blade, serrated on one edge. It's one of my favorite tools, excellent for weeding, cultivating, and digging small, deep holes. The serrated edge is used to saw woody stems.

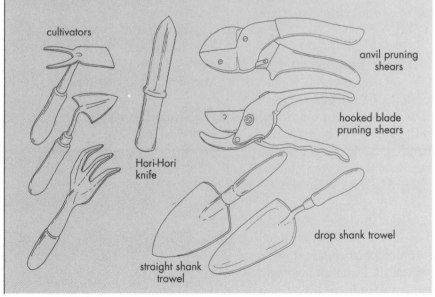

cultivators

Hori-Hori knife

straight shank trowel

anvil pruning shears

hooked blade pruning shears

drop shank trowel

Painted Gardening Gloves

Every gardener — and those whose only connection to the land is to mow the lawn — can use a pair of gloves to protect hard-working hands. Start with a plain pair of canvas or jersey gloves. Decorate with a colorful herb motif to create a lovely present guaranteed to get plenty of wear. Look at herbs with a new eye, and paint what you see.

MATERIALS

1 pair of plain canvas or jersey
  gloves, white or light color
Fabric paints
Brushes
1 squeeze-bottle fabric paint liner,
  black

1 Decide what you want to paint on the gloves. If you need to sketch on the gloves, do so in pencil. Don't paint on the palm of the glove, but by all means paint the back side (including the fingers) with your choice of colorful herbs and flowers.

2 Paint the basic shapes onto the gloves. (Try dill stems in gray-green, calendula flowers in orange, and chamomile stems and frilly leaves in bright green.)

3 When the basic shapes have dried, paint in the details — tiny yellow dots around the dill tops, green flower bases, for the calendula, and small white daisylike flowers with yellow centers for the calendula.

4 When the details have dried, use the squeeze bottle of fabric paint to outline each herb or flower and add any fine details you wish.

Gift Idea ❧

Children love to plant seeds and watch their progress. Many glove companies have begun to carry children's sizes. In early spring, give a child a gift of painted garden gloves; seed packets for easy-to-grow herbs, like parsley, calendula, and mint; a trowel; a box of cottonseed meal; and a booklet on growing herbs. This gift will last through the summer. Work with the child to till the soil, add the cottonseed meal, and plant the seeds. Help with transplanting, spacing, and harvesting. It doesn't take much space or money — this is really a gift of time!

Gardener's Gift Basket

Do you know an avid herb gardener, or someone just beginning to experiment with herbs? Whether you are a master gardener or a beginner yourself, you can put together a gardening basket. People love to get many small gifts centered on a theme; and they'll appreciate the thought you put into assembling it.

Choose a container. Baskets are lovely, and you can find some already plastic lined, for planting. (To prepare a basket yourself, line it in plastic lawn/leaf bags or heavier plastic, using a hot glue gun around the periphery to hold it in place.) The container can also be a large flowerpot or a decorative ceramic container, a large plastic or metal colander for rinsing freshly picked herbs, even a bucket for harvesting.

Buy some seed packets. If your gift is for someone who grows herbs, almost any herb will be a pleasure to receive. Maybe you can find an unusual variety that will grow in her region of the country.

Depending what you have selected thus far, choose other trinkets that fit. For potted plants, include a terra-cotta pot or a wooden planter, hand painted by you. You can also include a pair of hand-painted garden gloves, or a handmade plant marker for the type of seeds you bought. If you want to spend a bit more money, include a new garden trowel or cultivator, or a sun visor to keep her from getting sunburnt from all the time she's sure to spend outside gardening.

For someone who is just starting out, include a large bag of potting soil and a small bag of fertilizer. Label the material with the contents, so the recipient can learn more about making her own potting components.

Potting Soil Mix

3	parts sterilized soil or compost mix
1	part peat moss
1	part sand
¼	part fertilizer mix

Organic fertilizer mix

4	parts cottonseed or fish meal
1	part dolomite lime
1	part rock phosphate or bonemeal
1	part kelp meal

Finish it all up with a gift card. Include a quote about the joys of gardening. One of my favorites is this Chinese proverb: "He who plants a garden plants happiness."

Living Wreath

A living wreath is a wire frame, lined with moss and filled with fortified planting soil, with plant cuttings poked through the moss to allow them to grow roots in the soil. This is a long-term project — you do the work up front, and nature does the rest, at her own pace.

MATERIALS

2 halves of a half-round wire wreath form, 9″–10″ diameter
Sphagnum moss
Potting soil (recipe at right)
Cuttings of any of the following:
 Creeping sedum
 Creeping thyme
 Lateral rosemary
 Hens and chicks (houseleek)
 Lamb's ears
 Other perennial creeping herbs and rockery plants
Wire
U-shaped floral pins

EQUIPMENT

Bucket
Chopstick or skewer
12″ plastic tray or saucer

1 Soak the moss in a bucket of water for several hours.

2 Place the wire frames on your work surface so that the openings are face up. Line both frames with moss, creating a mat of moss to hold the soil in the frame.

3 Mix the *potting soil* (or use a highly fortified store-bought mix):

 3 parts sterilized soil or com- posted soil
 1 part peat moss
 1 part sand
 ½ part fertilizer, made of 4 parts cottonseed or fish meal; 1 part dolomite lime; 1 part rock phosphate or bonemeal; 1 part kelp meal

4 Moisten the soil mix and push as much of it as you can into each half of the mossy frame, slightly mounding the top of each.

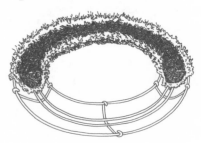

5 Quickly flip one frame over the other to form a moss-surrounded ring of soil. Wrap wire around the wreath at 1" intervals to hold it together.

6 Remove the cuttings from the soil, exposing the roots. Have the cuttings trimmed short, so that about 1" of stem can be pushed into the wreath. Lay the plants out in an attractive arrangement.

7 Starting toward the inside of the ring and working outward, poke a hole through the moss to the soil. Put one cutting in each hole. If the leafy part of the cutting is long enough to need securing to the moss, use a floral pin to hold it in place. Creeping plants will begin to root along their stems, too.

8 Continue poking and planting until the wreath is covered with plant material. Place the wreath into the plastic tray and pour water into it. The moss and soil will soak up the water.

9 Water weekly — more frequently if the moss feels dry. (Spray the surface with water if it seems very dry on top but moist on the bottom.) Continue to train the stems where you want them to root, using floral pins, all through the growing season. If you live in a cold climate, bring the wreath indoors for the winter; put it back out in the spring.

Once the wreath begins to thrive, it makes a lovely centerpiece for the table, with a candleholder or a bunch of flowers in the middle. Hang it on a door or wall; just remember to take it down and water it, allowing it to soak up as much water as it needs.

A Long-Lasting Gift ↝

My wreath is 5 years old now. The first year, the plant cuttings were establishing their roots; watering was my only job. It started to be genuinely beautiful during the summer of the second year. Since then I've taken cuttings from it and made more wreaths — it's prolific, and to keep it looking good, trimming is necessary. Trim off long stems, poke them into the soil, and anchor them into the moss. New roots will form.

Bucket Apron

The bucket apron is designed to fit around a 5-gallon pail. It allows you to carry tools, seeds, and marking pens with you through the garden, filling the bucket with weeds or harvested herbs or carrying fertilizers to spread in the soil. Note: Because the bucket apron has two large pockets (one on each side of the bucket), you must make two of everything.

MATERIALS

24 inches of 60″ wide or 1 yard of 44″ wide cotton canvas or twill
2 yards of cotton or nylon webbing, 1″ wide
4 yards of double-folded bias trim
Sewing thread
Two 1″ D-rings

EQUIPMENT

Sewing machine
Iron
Scissors

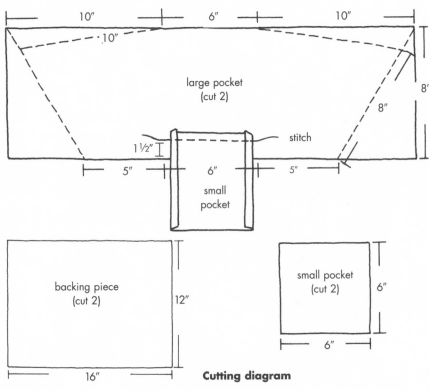

Cutting diagram

1 Follow the measurements on the cutting diagram to mark and cut the fabric. Notice that the upper edge of the large pocket is angled so that the sides measure 8″. Mark this shape on a piece of fabric 8″ high by 26″ wide, as shown. Mark the placement of the center pocket, with 5″ extensions on each side. Now, draw a diagonal from the end of each 5″ extension to each top corner. Measure 8″ up this diagonal line and complete the top edge as shown on the cutting diagram.

2 Sew bias binding to the top edge of each 6″ x 6″ pocket. Press under ½″ along the sides of each pocket. With right sides facing, place the pocket as shown, with its bottom edge 1½″ from the bottom edge of each large pocket. Stitch along stitching line. Fold the pocket up and iron it in place. Topstitch ⅛″ in from the side edges, backstitching at the pocket corners. Stitch again 1½″ in from one edge to make slots for pens and small tools.

3 Sew bias binding along the top edges of the large pockets. Lay a large pocket onto each backing piece, with the wrong side of the pocket facing the right side of the backing, and bottom edges aligned. Stitch along the bottom, using a ¼″ seam allowance.

4 With the assembled large pocket lying flat on the backing piece, pin the center of the pocket onto the backing. Measure 5″ in from each side edge and pin the small pocket flat to these points. Stitch, making a center (flat) pocket and two side (billowing) pockets. Line up the large pocket side edges with the backing side edges. Round the bottom corners, and stitch the pocket to the backing, using a ⅜″ seam allowance, following the rounded line around each corner.

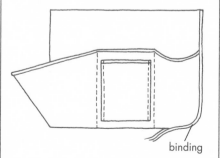

binding

5 Trim the bottom corners of the bags along the rounded shape. Starting at one upper corner, fold under the raw binding edge and sew binding around the sides and bottom of the bags, covering the seam allowances that connect the large pocket to the backing. Ease the binding around the curves and turn under the raw edge at the ending corner.

6 Press ½″ along the top of each backing piece toward the face of the fabric. Cut a 48″ length of webbing. Starting 3″ in from one end of the webbing, pin the webbing to the face of one of the apron bags (covering the pressed down edge). Stitch the webbing to the apron bag, ⅛″ in from each edge of the webbing. Leaving 2″ between apron bags, pin the webbing to the face of the second apron bag. Stitch as before.

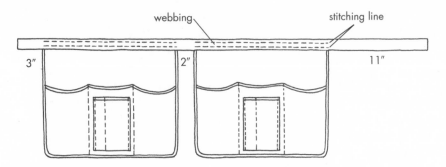

7 On the longer end of the strap of webbing, fold under 1" twice. Use a box stitch to finish the end.

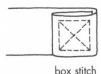

box stitch

8 Thread the two D-rings onto the 3" end of webbing. Fold under 1" twice and pin this to the back of the backing. This leaves the two D-rings on a ½" loop of webbing. Sew the folded ends to the backing with a box stitch.

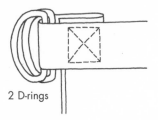

2 D-rings

9 Wrap the apron around the bucket. Thread the long strap through both D-rings, back through only one D-ring, and pull tight.

Apron Decoration ॐ

Trim apron pockets with colorful bias binding. Match colors to painted-on herbal motifs, such as sage leaves, sweet woodruff leaves and dainty flowers, and chive shoots with purple floral spheres.

CHAPTER 6

Gifts for the Home

The use of herbs, flowers, leaves, spices, and seeds to scent and decorate our homes has a long tradition. Before we became accustomed to buying manufactured items, people made their own candles, lamps, baskets, and other household necessities, often finding an opportunity for self-expression in the decoration of these objects. The projects in this chapter make use of several different techniques to make and adorn common household items, and can be adapted in many different ways.

Whether you stick with natural materials, such as hop vines and pressed flowers, or include technological advances like clock mechanisms and polymer clay, there are almost limitless possibilities for creating wonderful gifts. Imagine how precious a handmade lampshade on a beautiful base might be as a gift for a new bride, or the warm memories that might be evoked by a box of handmade Christmas ornaments. These gifts will stand the test of time and bring great joy to your friends and loved ones.

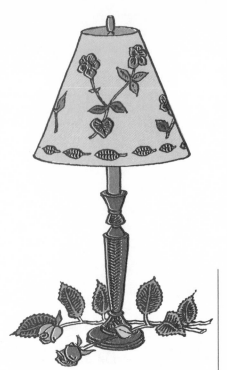

Herb-Decoupaged Lampshade

This project combines the technique of pressing leaves and flowers with decoupage. You can rejuvenate an old lampshade by speckling it with plant designs, or re-cover a lampshade frame with new shade material that you have decorated. See pages 6–7 for Leaf and Flower Press instructions.

MATERIALS

Watercolor paints and brushes (optional)
Pressed leaves and flowers
Lampshade
Decoupage medium (Mod-Podge or acrylic medium)
Flat brushes, 1″ and 3″
Fringe or beads (optional)
Hot glue gun (for fringe or beads)

Note: If you are decorating an old shade, be sure to choose one with a smooth finish.

1 Choose very flat plant material for this project. Sage, pansy, violet, bay, ginkgo, willow, oak, and individual petals from larger flowers, such as rose and poppy, work well. Press leaves and flowers until they are completely dry.

2 Some plants lose their color over time. Traditionally, flowers were painted before being sealed in wax or glass, to preserve their color. To do this, after pressing the plant material, mix watercolors or liquid artist inks. Using small brushes, paint the flowers and leaves to reflect their natural colors. Press them again until they are completely dry.

3 Brush small areas of the lampshade with decoupage medium, and affix the leaves and flowers as you please. Coat the outer surface of the plant material with medium, using broad strokes to blend the medium across the surface, rather than creating a thick layer of medium over each leaf.

4 Add leaves and flowers until you are finished with your design. When the first coat of sealer is dry, use the 3″ brush to coat the entire surface in long, broad strokes. Coat several more times, allowing the sealer to dry thoroughly between applications.

5 Decorate the bottom edge of the lampshade with fringe or beads, using a hot glue gun to attach them.

Making a New Lampshade

If you have a round frame with a shade in need of replacement, here's how to make a new shade or cover an old one.

MATERIALS
Round lampshade frame
Vellum (heavyweight coated tracing paper)

EQUIPMENT
Ruler
Hot glue gun or very tacky craft glue
Scissors
Fringe or other decorative trim

1 If you have the old shade, remove it from the frame carefully and trace it onto the vellum, adding ½″ to the end for your new shade to overlap. If you don't have the old shade, wrap the vellum around the

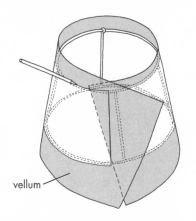

vellum

frame. Trace the lines along the top and bottom rings of the frame. Using the ruler as a guide, draw a straight line down the height of the frame near one end of the vellum.

2 Remove vellum from frame, smooth out your sketching lines, and cut along the top and bottom frame's traced lines. Cut along single height line, leaving other end long. Wrap the new shade around the frame again (you may want to tape it on temporarily with masking tape), and make sure that the upper and lower edges match well. Overlap the long end over the cut end, and draw a line where they overlap ½″. Remove vellum and trim end.

3 You can decorate this frame flat on a table, or attach it to the frame now.

4 To attach shade to frame, brush tacky glue or squeeze hot glue along frame uprights and rings, and carefully place shade onto the frame, starting at a metal upright so that the seam will be over a metal rod. Brush a ½″ strip of glue onto one end of the vellum and overlap the other end to complete the circle.

5 After you have decorated the shade, and have applied at least 3–6 layers of sealer/medium to make the shade water resistant, glue trim along the top and bottom circumferences of the shade, to hide the raw edges of the vellum.

½″ overlap for gluing

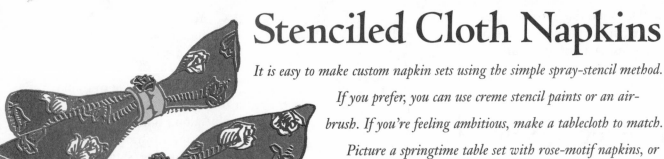

Stenciled Cloth Napkins

It is easy to make custom napkin sets using the simple spray-stencil method.

If you prefer, you can use creme stencil paints or an air-

brush. If you're feeling ambitious, make a tablecloth to match.

Picture a springtime table set with rose-motif napkins, or

a holiday buffet set with holly leaf and berry theme.

MATERIALS

White or pastel napkins, or fabric

Fabric paints (or airbrush fabric inks)

EQUIPMENT

Several spray bottles

Store-bought stencils or stencil paper, cardboard, or acetate

X-acto or mat knife

Iron

Small paintbrushes (for adding detail)

Newspaper or other absorbent work surface

Hole punch

1 If you are starting with fabric, cut 14″ squares of fabric and zigzag or serge (serging is an overedge stitch that conceals the edge of the fabric) the edges to prevent fabric edge from raveling.

2 Launder the napkins to remove the sizing; then iron them.

3 To make your own stencils, cut the stencil paper 2″ larger than the napkin on each edge. Draw the design onto the stencil paper, cardboard, or acetate and carefully cut out the shapes, to create the composition of the whole napkin. Make a separate stencil for each color you intend

to spray. If the stencils need to line up a certain way, place them on top of each other aligned correctly, and use a hole punch or knife to make registration holes in exactly the same location through all the layers.

4 You will be using washes of paint — thin enough to spray through a plastic spray bottle, but thick enough not to bleed. Put about ½ cup of water into a bottle and add a few tablespoons of paint. Shake well, and test spray onto paper or scrap cloth. Continue adding paint until the color is as thick as it can be and still spray through the tube. Repeat this process for all the colors you'll be using. For my roses and leaves, I'm using two shades of pink for the petals and a gray/green for the leaves.

5 On the work surface, draw the napkin exactly to size. Place the first napkin into this outline. Place the first stencil on the first napkin and spray lightly into the open spaces. Also spray through the registration holes, which will mark the work surface. Allow this first spray to dry slightly, then spray again, until you have built up the color depth.

6 Carefully move this napkin to a safe place to dry. Place the next napkin on the outline and stencil it; repeat until you have sprayed the first color onto all of your napkins.

7 Place the driest napkin into the outline and line up the second stencil with the registration marks. Repeat the process with each color stencil until all of the napkins are done.

8 If you want to add detail, like the shadows between the petals, for example, use a small brush with full-strength paint.

9 When they are dry, iron the napkins to cure the paint, according to the manufacturer's instructions.

A Rosy Ring ❧

You can use wrapped floral wire to fashion a napkin ring and tuck a rosebud and a few herb sprigs into each one along with the napkin.

Garden-Theme Switch Plates

Plain plastic or wooden switch plates can be adorned in many ways. This project involves covering the switch plate with a polymer clay design. Beads, sequins, or other decorative trinkets may be added to the clay. You can also decorate switch plates using paints or decoupage, as explained in the second version.

MATERIALS

Plastic or wooden switch plate
Sandpaper, medium grit
Tacky glue
Several colors of polymer clay
Water-based varnish

EQUIPMENT

Straight-sided bottle or rolling pin
Skewer or sharp knife
Cookie sheet or glass pie plate
Paintbrush

1 With the sandpaper, "rough up" the surface of the switch plate. This will help the clay to adhere. If, after you have oven-cured the clay and switch plate, the clay will not stick to the switch plate, use tacky glue to permanently affix the clay design to the plate. Having been oven-cured on the switch plate, it should now fit perfectly.

2 Roll out your background color to a thickness of about ⅛″ and push it onto the switch plate. Cut through the switch holes and push a skewer through the screw holes. (Make the holes large enough for the heads of the screws to fit through, so they can be tightened down to the surface of the switch plate.) Trim the edges of the clay flush with the edges of the switch plate.

3 Make the design with polymer clay, using herbs like violas (great leaf shape), rue (blue-green color), or rosemary in full bloom (green needles with purple florets). The design can protrude slightly from the surface, but try to keep it relatively flat near the openings for the switches, since people will be reaching for them in the dark and may break the clay parts. You can extend up to 1″ beyond the edges of the switch plate with the clay, but you should lay a piece of wire into the clay, extending through the length of the protruding piece, to prevent it from breaking off.

4 If you use beads, sequins, or other materials, anchor them securely in the clay. Use items

that can withstand 20 minutes in a 275°F oven.

5 When you are finished, oven-cure the clay on the switch plate according to the manufacturer's instructions.

6 When cool, coat with 2 layers of clear varnish for a finished surface.

Decoupaged Switch Plates

Those empty seed packets and old seed and garden catalogs you saved are coming in handy once again! Beautiful photos of herbs or old-fashioned seed packets can add real charm to a kitchen or pantry light switch. These are easy to make, and they're great as gifts.

MATERIALS

Paper materials for decoupage
Plastic or wooden switch plate
Decoupage medium, such as
  Mod-Podge or acrylic medium
1″ flat brush
X-acto or mat knife

1 Cut images from catalogs, or cut the fronts off seed packets. Arrange them on the switch plate until you have a composition you like. Make sure that the images extend ½″ beyond the edge of the switch plate, so that you can fold them under the switch plate to make clean-finished edges.

2 Coat the switch plate with decoupage medium, and affix the paper images, covering each with a coat of medium. The paper pieces should overlap to completely cover the plastic or wood. Coat the edges and a border around the back of the switch plate with medium, use the brush to push the paper around the edges, and seal them to the back of the switch plate. (If you don't have decoupage medium, the paper can be affixed with white glue and then painted with several coats of water-based varnish.)

3 Turn over the switch plate. With a knife, cut out the switch holes. Use the knife point or a skewer to open the screw holes.

Variations ∾

∾ Decoupaging pressed plant materials (as in the lampshade project) can also be interesting.

∾ If you have a number of switch plates in a kitchen or hallway, decorate each with a different herb packet.

∾ Make a small protruding loop of clay on the lower edge of the switch plate, using wire covered in clay, and keep a tiny bunch of dried flowers or herbs in it.

4 Allow the decoupage to dry. Paint the entire front and edges of the switch plate with another coat of decoupage medium.

Herb-Printed Scented Clock

Clocks make great gifts; they're consulted frequently throughout the day and are part of a room's decor. You don't have to be an expert woodworker to make this one, though you will need a few tools. See pages 113–115 for nature printing techniques.

MATERIALS

¾" pine or other light-colored wood, 10" x 10"

Clock mechanism with ¾" shaft, and hands

Water-based printing inks and extender

Flat-pressed leaves for printing

Scented wood finish cream (instructions follow)

EQUIPMENT

Pencil

Ruler

Compass

Hand coping saw or electric jigsaw

Drill, drill bit to fit clock shaft

Sandpaper, medium- and fine-grit

Printing equipment (see pages 113–115)

2" flat brush

Clean rags

1 Using a compass, draw a 10" diameter circle on the wood, marking the center with pencil. Cut out the circle with a saw.

2 When you purchase the clock mechanism, you will order by shaft length and diameter, so you will know what size drill bit to get. Use a drill bit that is slightly larger than the shaft dimension. Instructions on clock assembly will be included from the supplier. Drill a straight hole in the center of the wood. Insert the clock shaft, to verify the hole is the right diameter and length. Remove the mechanism so you can decorate the clock face.

3 Sand the edges of the circle with medium-grit sandpaper. Finish sanding with fine-grit paper.

4 Using the compass set at the same radius as the original circle, make a very light pencil mark anywhere on the periphery of the circle. Put the compass pointer on this mark and swing the pencil around to mark where it hits the circumference of the circle. Now put the pointer on the second mark, and mark the next point with the pencil. Continue this until there are six marks, numbered on the drawing.

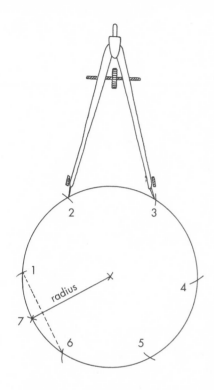

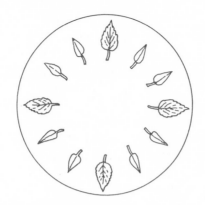

5 Using a ruler, locate a point halfway between two of the marks and extend this point from the center out to the edge of the circle (7). Using this point to start, proceed around the circle using the compass to mark the six points halfway between the first six points. You have now located the 12 hours of the day.

6 Using the roller and simple leaf shapes (the same or different ones for each of the clock's numerals), ink a leaf, and print at each of the 12 marks on the circle. If you like, use a larger leaf for the 12, 3, 6, and 9. Test-print on a scrap of wood first to adjust the amount of ink before you print directly on the clock.

7 Test the finish on the printed wood scrap, to be sure that it will not react adversely with the ink you have used. (Since you have to make the wood finish 2 weeks before using it, it would be advisable to print a leaf, allow it to dry, and do this wood finish test before printing your clock. If the ink smudges, find a different ink for printing.) If all the components are compatible, apply a thin layer of the scented finish to the clock face and sides with a flat brush or rag. Allow this to soak in for 20 minutes. Rub the finish in with a clean, soft cloth, to heat the wood and allow more finish to flow into the wood pores. Avoid rubbing the printed areas.

8 Refinish the wood once a month (time to allow the beeswax to dry thoroughly between coats) for 3–6 months to build up a deep and lustrous finish, and add scent to the wood. Or give the gift with the jar of finish, with instructions for refinishing the wood monthly. Remove the hands to facilitate refinishing.

9 Insert the clock mechanism through the drilled hole and attach the hands according to the manufacturer's instructions. Insert batteries.

Scented Wood Finish

Work in a well-ventilated area!

INGREDIENTS

Makes 1 quart

- 1 ounce beeswax
- 1 pint raw linseed oil
- 1 pint turpentine
- For scents: either 40 sweet cicely seeds, chopped and crushed
  or
- 1 teaspoon each lemon and lime essential oil
  or
- 1½ teaspoons lavender oil plus 4 drops peppermint oil

EQUIPMENT

Double boiler
Cheesecloth or stocking
Wide-mouthed jar with lid

1 Melt the beeswax in a microwave or double boiler.

2 Remove it from the heat and stir in the oil and turpentine.

3 Strain the mixture through doubled cheesecloth or a nylon stocking.

4 Pour the mixture into a wide-mouthed jar that has a lid. Allow to cool before covering.

5 Add the seeds or essential oils as it is cooling.

6 When cool, cover with a tight-fitting lid. Allow it to cure for 2 weeks, shaking occasionally. The scent of the turpentine will diminish during this time.

Herbal Lore: Sweet Cicely ∾

This herb is a hardy, shade-loving perennial with a scent like lovage. The leaf flavor is that of a sweet anise, and it can be used as garnish, in salads, or as a sweetener to cut down the acidity of fruit. Treat the roots, which are antiseptic, as you would parsnip. The seeds are shiny, brown, and up to 1″ long, with a spicy licorice flavor, and have been traditionally used in candy, cakes, and liqueurs. The roots or seeds can be candied. In the wood finish recipe, the seeds will produce a licorice-scented oil finish.

To make your own liqueur, follow the instructions on page 41 (with Painted Vinegar Bottles), using ¼ cup sweet cicely seeds per batch.

Polymer Clay Wall Vase

Here is an excellent project for adults or children. The decorative polymer clay exterior conceals a glass jar that can be hung on the wall and used as a vase for tiny fresh-cut herbs or flowers. The size of the jar determines the size of the flowers; a small jar would hold violets, pansies, lavender, rosemary, chamomile, thyme, or johnny jump-ups.

MATERIALS

Polymer clay
Small glass jar
Water-based varnish

EQUIPMENT

Rolling pin or round wooden dowel
Pencil or skewer
Glass baking dish
Oven
Small flat paintbrush

1 Roll out a sheet of polymer clay 3⁄16″–1⁄4″ thick. This is the back of the vase, which will lie flat against the wall. Make it twice the height of the jar. Use a pencil or skewer to poke a hole through the clay at least 1⁄2″ down from the top, for hanging.

2 Place the jar on its side on the lower half of the clay backing. Roll clay ropes, and braid or weave them. Place the interlaced clay over the jar to look like a basket. Push each row of braid, or "thread" of the weave, up against the previous one, to close any holes that might reveal the jar. Push the clay up around the lip of the jar to hide it.

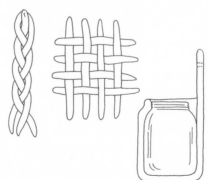

3 Decorate the basket and backing with tiny clay flowers or insects or other decorative shapes.

4 Lay the finished vase in the glass dish, and oven-cure the clay according to the manufacturer's instructions.

5 When it's cool, brush on several coats of varnish, allowing it to dry between coats.

6 Fill the jar 3⁄4 full of water, add some fresh herbs and flowers, and hang it from a nail on the wall. (You can also use it for dried herbs; just don't put water in the jar.)

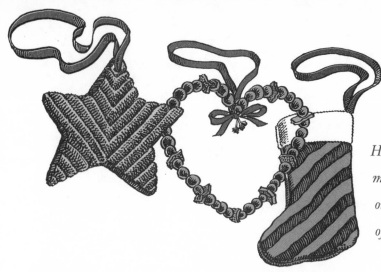

Holiday Ornaments

Here are three suggestions for combining fresh materials to make fragrant and attractive holiday ornaments. They'll fill your home with the aroma of the season, or you can give them as gifts.

Apple-Cinnamon Scented Cutouts

These ornaments last for years, exuding the luscious scent of spicy apples. They are not edible.

MATERIALS

1½ cups applesauce
1½ cups cinnamon, ground
Extra cinnamon
Ribbon (⅛″–¼″ wide)

EQUIPMENT

Mixing bowl and spoon
Waxed paper
Rolling pin
Cookie cutters
Toothpick

1 Mix the applesauce with the cinnamon. Add more applesauce if the mixture is dry; add more cinnamon if it's too mushy. Let sit at room temperature for 2–3 hours.

2 Sprinkle cinnamon on a sheet of waxed paper. Place the dough on the cinnamon; then sprinkle with more cinnamon. Roll out the dough to a thickness of at least ¼″.

3 Use cookie cutters to cut shapes. Poke a hole in the top of each to thread a ribbon after they are dry. With a toothpick, texture the surface of the dough.

4 Dry the finished shapes at room temperature for 3–4 days. Thread ribbon through the hole in each piece to hang them as ornaments or attach to a decorative wreath.

Variation: Roll the dough into small balls, 1½″ in diameter. When dry, wrap them in lace or netting, tied shut, and make a loop with ribbon. Glue some dried flowers or berries along the ribbon, and hang from the tree for scent and decoration.

Wired Fruit Decorations

MATERIALS

Cranberries
Citrus fruit peels
22-gauge wire
¼"-wide ribbon
Dried flowers or leaves (such as
  oregano florets or bay leaves)

EQUIPMENT

Sharp knife or vegetable peeler
Glue gun or tacky glue

1 Use cranberries just as they come from the package. For citrus fruit, pare the outer peel from the fruit. Cut the strips into approximately 1" squares.

2 Shape the wire into hearts about 4" across, with the wire ends at the top center of the heart. Push the cranberries and peels tightly onto the wire. They will shrink as they dry.

3 Twist the wire ends together to close the heart. Use the ribbon to cover the wire, make a loop for hanging, and tie a decorative bow at the center of the heart. Glue on dried flowers or leaves, if desired.

4 Hang the ornament to dry for several weeks.

You can also make wreath decorations using dried apple slices (see page 19).

Scented Sachet Ornaments

Hang spicy sachet bags from your tree, or make stocking-shaped ornaments filled with pine, cedar, or spice potpourri. Here is a basic mixture.

INGREDIENTS

2 quarts pine needles
1 cup cut orrisroot
1 tablespoon pine oil

Holiday Room Scent ✑

This mixture — simmered on the stove on low heat or over a wood fire — makes the house smell wonderful.

2 cups water
1 teaspoon allspice
1 teaspoon whole cloves
6 cinnamon sticks
1 tablespoon rosemary
4–5 drops vanilla extract

Add more water periodically as needed.

Instead of the pine base, you can use rose petals, mint leaves, lemon verbena, whole cinnamon, cloves, nutmeg, cedar chips, bay leaves, dried citrus peels, broken vanilla beans, or oils other than pine.

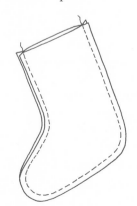

Hop-Vine Basket

Hop vines can grow up to 25 feet in length, so it won't take many plants to make this project. Use this basket to hold a pot of herbs or flowers, or line it with sphagnum moss, fill it with potting soil, and plant through holes in the moss as a living, hanging container.

MATERIALS

Hop vines (grow hop from seeds or buy plant starts, both available from nurseries)
Can or jar, 4"–5" in diameter
Florist's wire
12 strands of heavy raffia, each at least 1 yard long

1 Form the vines into 6 or 8 separate rings around the can, joining the ends with a wrapping of wire. Dry in place at least 2 weeks. Remove the rings from the can.

2 Knot a piece of raffia on the first ring by folding it in half, slipping the loop around a ring, and slipping the ends of the raffia back through the loop. Pull tight. Space five more loops of raffia around the ring.

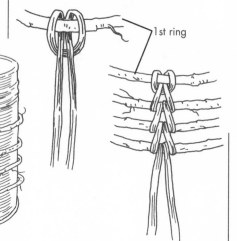

1st ring

3 Stack another ring of vine under the first and pull each strand of raffia from the first ring over the outside of the second. Wrap the raffia around the ring and back through the loop it formed. Continue with all six strands of raffia, locating one directly over the wire wrap of each ring. Add rings until you have used up all the rings.

4 Gather the raffia ends into a bundle at the base of the basket and tie in a single knot close to the basket bottom.

5 To make the hanger, with the same loop knot used in step 2, tie the remaining raffia strands to the top of the basket in pairs, evenly spaced at three points around the basket. Knot these strands together in the exact center, 8″ above the basket. For a hanging loop, tie a second knot above the first. Pull the knots tight. Trim the excess raffia 1″ beyond the top knot and 3″ beyond the bottom knot. *Note:* If you want to plant directly into the hop-vine basket (see below), make the hop-vine basket larger by starting with larger diameter rings made from longer lengths of vine, and fasten together with more strands of raffia laced to make a strong, relatively closely woven grid. Leave spaces between the raffia large enough for the root crowns or stems of the plants you intend to use.

About Potless Hanging Baskets

Any openwork basket (such as this hop-vine basket) or wire form can be used for planting. Line it with sphagnum moss and fill with potting soil. Poke holes through the moss and insert the roots of your favorite herbs. By planting herb starts through the moss into the soil from all sides of the basket, there is an impen-

Crocheted Baskets ❧

If you know how to crochet, you can create a hanging basket out of twine with a large crochet hook. These baskets can be harvest totes or grocery bags, too. The finished look is similar to macrame, but you work in circles with a single strand rather than in rows using multiple strands.

Jute twine is durable and has an earthy feel. Jute is a bast fiber, as are linen, hemp, sisal, and ramie. Synthetic twines last longer and are more mildew resistant than natural ones. They also come in colors, so you can make more decorative baskets.

Start with a chain of three or four loops and loop them

together in a circle. Single crochet around the circle, with two stitches in each chain, to increase the circumference of the circle. When you have a flat circle as large as you want your basket base, continue to single crochet with one stitch per chain. This will begin to build straight walls up the sides of the basket.

You can hang the basket from three or four chain-stitched lengths, attached to the top row, knotted at the top to form a hanging loop. Using twine and a large needle should create a texture with holes big enough to poke plants through — adjust your needle size and tension to the texture you desire.

etrable wall around the soil. Plant some herb starts in the top soil too. Keep the soil well watered, top and bottom.

Baskets of commonly used cooking herbs like parsley, cilantro, mizuna, mesclun lettuce mix, sorrel, basil, and other

leafy greens are wonderful to have hanging right outside the kitchen door. Pull off a few leaves at a time; the plants will send out more new shoots all summer. Don't forget to water them!

Firestarters

Used as kindling over newspaper in the fireplace or woodstove — or to start the campfire in the woods — these fragrant firestarters are made from recycled materials. Pair them with a decoupaged matchbox filled with long wooden matches and present them as a housewarming gift for friends who have their first fireplace.

Pinecone Firestarters

MATERIALS

Egg carton
Sawdust or dried herbs (rosemary or
  lavender works well)
Pinecones
Paraffin, old candle ends, or candle
  wax with 135°–145°F melting point
Ribbon (optional)

EQUIPMENT

Kraft paper or sheets of unprinted
  scrap paper
Double boiler
Mixing bowl or coffee can
Knife or scissors

1 Cover your work area with kraft paper or other unprinted paper.

2 Put some sawdust or dried herbs in each compartment of the egg carton and work a pinecone firmly into the sawdust.

3 Melt the wax in the top of a double boiler. Use a bowl that you intend for wax and craft projects, now and forever, or set a coffee can on a metal trivet in a large pot of water for a makeshift double boiler. (See instructions for the double boiler included in the Herbal Candle project on pages 102–104.)

4 Pour wax over each pinecone in the egg carton, coating thoroughly. As it cools, if the wax level drops, add more melted wax.

5 When the wax has cooled, cut the egg carton into individual firestarters. Tie a ribbon around each pinecone, if desired.

Wood Chip, Herb, and Sawdust Firestarters

Rosemary or lavender branches, chopped up, work well in these balls. Firestarters can be stored indefinitely in a cool place.

MATERIALS
2 pounds paraffin (candle ends work well)
3 cups dry wood chips and sawdust
1 cup dried herbs for scent, or cedar and pine needles

EQUIPMENT
Double boiler
Old bowl
Old wooden spoon or stick
Rubber gloves
Newspaper or metal tray

1 Melt the candle ends in the top of a double boiler.

2 Put the wood chips, herbs, and sawdust in an old bowl or plastic bin. Pour the wax over the wood and stir. The more wood you can work into the wax, the better they will burn.

3 Wearing rubber gloves, work the wax and wood together while the wax is still warm (but not so hot that it burns your hands). Form the mixture into balls, about 2″ in diameter.

4 Place the balls on newspaper or a metal tray to cool.

Herbal Candles

*This project involves decorating a store-bought candle with
dried herbs and overdipping it with a thin film of paraffin.
If you'd like to explore the wonders of candlemaking, read*
The Candlemaker's Companion *(see page 124).*

MATERIALS

Pillar candle, 3″ or more in diameter
Spray adhesive or white glue
Dried herbs (or potpourri mix)
**Paraffin, 135°–145°F melting point
(not canning paraffin)**
Candle scent or essential oil

EQUIPMENT

Small flat brush
Tweezers
Double boiler
Thermometer (0°–200°F)
Bucket
Pliers
Ice pick

1 Spray the candle with the
adhesive and attach the leaves
and flowers. Or brush the leaves
and flowers with white glue, and
use tweezers to place them on
the candle. To attach finely

crushed potpourri, coat the sides
of the candle with white glue and
roll the candle in a layer of
potpourri. Do not put plant
material on the top of the candle, as it may catch fire.

2 Set up the double boiler as
shown. To heat the water, use a
large pot with a metal trivet
inside it, to raise the wax can so
that water can flow underneath
it. To melt the paraffin, use a
container that is taller than the
candle. Melt enough wax to submerge the candle. The candle
will displace wax, and the container must be deep enough not
to overflow when the candle is
pushed down into it. A 4″-high
pillar works well with a 5-pound

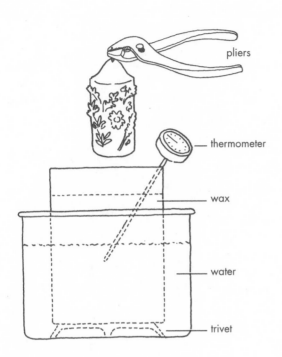

pliers

thermometer

wax

water

trivet

coffee can. For anything larger, try a large olive oil can, or purchase a wax melting can from a candle supplier. Put the wax into the can and place the can into the pot. Fill the pot with water so that it comes up as high as possible without causing the can of wax to float. Turn on the heat, and wait for the wax to melt and reach a temperature of about 150°F.

3 Fill a bucket ¾ full of cool water, and have it near the wax.

4 Grab the wick of the decorated candle with pliers and submerge the candle in the 150°F wax. Pull it out slowly, taking particular care to allow the wax to flow slowly over the top and sides. You don't want large drips. Immediately submerge the candle in the water.

Decorative Candleholders ∾

Decorate candleholders with small wreaths of plant material, which sit on the lip of a taper holder or around the edge of a plate holding a pillar. Start with a wire ring the size of, or slightly smaller than, the full circumference of your holders. Attach dried herb sprigs and flowers, such as lavender, oregano, and sage, using wire or a hot glue gun, working on both sides of the wire so that the candle will be surrounded by foliage. You can also glue or tie bows to the wreaths. Place the wreath around the candle.

5 Make sure all of the water is off the candle and repeat the waxing process. If you had wax drips from the first coating, you should be able to even them out by pulling out more smoothly the second time. Plunge the candle into the water. This makes it shiny, and cools and hardens it quickly.

6 For a scented candle, place a drop of scented oil into the pool of liquid wax that forms around the lighted wick.

Or give a scented candle kit as a gift. With the candle, pack a bottle of scented oil, an ice pick and a decorative card with these directions: Heat the ice pick over a flame and poke five or six holes about 1″ deep around the top of the candle. Drop scented oil into the holes and light the candle. For more scent, add a drop of the oil to the pool of wax.

Note: Never leave burning candles unattended. Candles decorated with flammable materials are particularly dangerous. A 3″-diameter or larger candle is recommended for this project because the flame and hot wax rarely reach the outer surface of these large pillars, thus decreasing the chances of the decorations catching fire. Exercise caution, though. A small draft can push the flame toward one side of the candle.

Recycling Old Candle Ends ∾

Save the ends of all the candles you burn. Melt them in a double boiler and pour through medium-weight sewable interfacing or muslin, to catch the wicks, metal tabs, and other debris. Pour the clean wax into an old metal baking pan that has been brushed with vegetable oil. When it cools, pop the wax out of the pan. If all of your candles are white, your wax chunks will be pure white. If you burn beeswax, you can keep it separate and filter pure beeswax for reuse in cosmetic and candle projects. Most of the time, when mixing waxes, the resulting recycled wax will be a reddish brown color, and can be used for things like the firestarters on pages 100–101.

CHAPTER 7

Techniques

This section will provide you with background information on techniques used within the text. Many of the projects suggest a decorative technique, but I encourage you to read through this section so that your creative juices might inspire you to combine, alter, or embellish the suggestions I have made. Also included are some guidelines for creating your own potpourris and other blends, so you can get an understanding of what key elements make the mixtures work. Information on art materials, including brushes and paints, will guide you in determining what to buy once you decide what you want to make.

The final section covers wrapping gifts, a finishing touch I hope you will enjoy. There are many ways to adorn a simple gift, not only with decorative wrap, but also with useful information and small, thoughtful additions that make the gift a heartfelt and memorable offering.

BUYING HERBS AND OTHER PLANT MATERIALS

The Source List on pages 117–118 includes suppliers of materials used for potpourris, tea and herbal blends, and essential oil blends. Most plant materials are sold in several forms: whole, cut, and powdered. In many decorative applications, powder is not recommended; it will seep through fabric bags. If you want to dissolve the herb, or want as little texture as possible, you will be using the powder or essential oil form. Each recipe in this book indicates which form to use.

Try growing herbs and flowers on your own. Many herbs do well in pots on a small urban apartment balcony or fire escape. After all, most of them are "weeds" that we humans have decided to utilize. You can start them in egg cartons indoors, and transplant them outside when the weather warms. There's nothing quite like using fresh herbs for cooking, and the rewards of making gifts from homegrown plants cannot be overstated — it's economical and emotionally satisfying.

Even the most accomplished gardener will have to purchase some items. Perusing the herb catalogs is fun and informative — many of them include recipes and projects as well.

DRYING HERBS AND FLOWERS AT HOME

Harvest on a dry day, in the morning, after the dew has dried. If you have the foresight to spray them clean the day before you plan to pick them, you won't have to rinse them the morning you harvest. Herbs on stems (most of the leafy greens, such as oregano, thyme, and mint) can be bundled with twine or wire and hung in a cool dark place for a week or two.

Separate leaves and flowers are easily dried on a window screen propped up for air circulation. Move the plant material around every day or so; that way the damp side can be shifted upward and will dry faster.

Once the materials are dried completely, store them in sealed jars or in zip-seal bags, labeled with the name and date (use the oldest product first). During the spring and summer, I harvest whatever is ready, and keep a continuous drying process going for 6 months!

For pressing flowers and leaves in a special press, refer to the directions on pages 6–7. You can also press plant material with phone books or other heavy volumes. Layer the plant material between paper towels or unprinted newsprint, and change the paper at least once a day. Moister plants may need to have the paper changed every 12 hours for the first few days.

MAKING WATER INFUSIONS AND TEAS

Generally, infusions and teas should be made just before you use them. They are usually cooled to room temperature and then combined into the recipe. Often, they have some scent and flavor (although they are not always edible), but for a highly scented product, essential oils are added for their concentrated aroma. Heating the plant material, or steeping it for a length of time, causes the plant fiber to release its healing compounds into the liquid.

For a basic infusion, add 1 cup of boiling water to 1 table-

spoon dried (¼ cup fresh) herbs or flowers. Allow it to steep until it cools. Strain the plant material through muslin, cheesecloth, or a coffee filter placed in a strainer.

Making Infused Oils

Infused oils are not the same as essential oils. By steeping the plant material in oil, you draw the plant's natural oils (the plant's essential oils) into the carrier oil and create a diluted form of the plant oil. Cover several handfuls of herbs or flowers with oil (sweet almond, grape seed, apricot kernel, jojoba, or a quality olive or other vegetable oil). Heat the oil in the top of a double boiler until the plant material wilts. Cool the mixture, uncovered. Remove the herbs, using muslin or cheesecloth in a strainer (coffee filters won't strain oil very well), but do not press the plant material or the oil will become cloudy. Allow the oil to drip through at its own pace. Warm the oil over low heat for 1–2 hours, uncovered, to evaporate any water and to eliminate the possibility of bacterial growth. Recent studies have shown that storing plant material in oil can be dangerous if there is any moisture at all in the plant. Bottle the plant-free oil. Use for cooking, massage, or in cosmetics.

BLENDING WITH ESSENTIAL OILS

Essential oils are rarely used full strength. In fact, some of them are so concentrated that they can irritate or even poison you. Research the material before using it. There are very few essential oils that can be used full strength on the skin (lavender is an exception), and in general, essential oils are so strong that they hardly smell like the scent we're used to — they must be diluted to be palatable.

There are many products on the market that call themselves essential oils but are really synthetic or diluted forms of the oil. Pure essential oils are expensive and come in dark-colored glass bottles. The price varies for each plant type, based on oil yield per plant and availability of materials. The suppliers listed in the Source List on pages 117–118 will provide you with high-quality oils.

When working with essential oils, use an eyedropper and count the number of drops. These oils are so concentrated that a slip of the dropper can overwhelm a recipe.

Documenting what you have done will be invaluable the next time you decide to make the product, or when you want to modify a recipe that perhaps turned out too weak or too strong. Maintain a notebook and refer to it often — you'll be glad you did.

Essential oils are generally used in 1–3 percent dilutions. For bath and body products, dilution in carrier oils is standard; sometimes this is the finished product (as with massage or bath oil); at other times the diluted oil becomes an ingredient for a cream or lotion. Common carrier oils are sweet almond, grape seed, apricot kernel, and jojoba. A 10 percent addition of avocado or wheat germ oil may be part of the recipe for skin conditioning. Vitamins A and E (liquid oils, commonly found in gel caps at the pharmacy) can be added for further skin nutrition.

A general guideline for diluting essential oils is to use 6–15 drops of essential oil to 1 tablespoon of carrier oil. This

makes ½ fluid ounce of dilute material — enough for a full body massage.

For potpourri, you will be dropping the oils directly onto the fixatives, herbs, and flowers for absorption into the blend.

NOTES ON POTPOURRI

There are thousands of variations of potpourri. The basic formula is as follows:

1 Main scent: This is your personal preference, or what you have available. It is generally a floral, fruity, or earthy scent, like lavender, rose, citrus, or patchouli.

2 Fixative: These specific plants and resins have a natural ability to hold the scent and are essential, since they make the scent last and last:

Roots: orris, calamus, vetiver
Gums and resins: benzoin, frankincense, myrrh, balsam
Plant and cellulosic fiber: processed corn cob, cedar, sandalwood, oak moss
Animal: musk, ambergris, civet, castorium

3 Blenders: These are other flavors and scents that are added to enhance and complement the main scent.

4 Oils: Begin with an oil of the main scent and augment with complementary scents.

5 Bulk: You can achieve bulk using oak moss, cedar, or citrus peels, all of which will also act as fixatives. Add bulky, colorful flowers and leaves for a pretty display. For some applications, bulk is not desired, so this ingredient can be omitted.

A basic blend is 2 cups of blended fragrant flowers, herbs, and spices; ¼ cup fixative; and 20 drops of essential oil.

I have included various recipes throughout the book, some simple, others quite complex and costly to assemble. If you remain aware of the five basic ingredients of potpourri, you will be able to add or delete specific ingredients without losing the key aspects of a quality potpourri.

Powders tend to seep through fabric bags, so use chips or whole flowers, particularly in sachet and pillow applications.

On Notebooks ✍

I am a firm believer in note keeping. I never assume that I will remember a recipe. I write down the following kinds of things:

✍ What ingredients did I use?

✍ What quantities of each ingredient did I use, and in what order?

✍ Where did I buy any unusual ingredients?

✍ How long, and at what temperature, did I cook/cool the mixture?

✍ How did the end product turn out?

✍ What would I change the next time I make it?

These notes have been invaluable over the years. They avert the frustration that can result when you try to reproduce a recipe, color, or scent.

Some people experience an allergic reaction to orrisroot. The newest cellulosic fiber fixatives, made from processed corn cob, seem to cause fewer problems.

Notes on Paints and Inks

There are so many paints on the market that it would be impossible to list them all. However, they can be easily divided into water-based (including acrylic, latex, some inks) and oil-based types. Within each category, paints are labeled interior, exterior, enamel, gloss, semi-gloss, satin, etc. If you choose a water-based paint, the cleanup is easily accomplished with soap and water. For most applications, you will be able to find a water-based paint to fit your needs. For durability and rustproofing, you may want to use an oil-based paint. Read the directions to determine the exact solvent needed (paint thinner, lacquer thinner, turpentine, acetone), and work in a well-ventilated area. There are some new citrus-based solvents that are less toxic than the traditional chemical solvents, but you will have to read carefully or experiment to determine whether this will work with the paint you have chosen. Never mix water-based and oil-based products.

As a general rule, when working on paper, use watercolor paints or water-based inks.

For wood, you can use acrylics, latex, or oil-based paints. Wood may require a base coat of primer to seal the grain and allow the colors to go on evenly. Ceramics can be painted with any of the acrylics or oil-based paints, and there is also a water-based ceramic paint, available in craft stores. You can paint on fabric with acrylics, but the paint will tend to sit on the surface of the fabric and not be absorbed into the fibers. You'll have better results using fabric paints, dyes, or inks; these impart a softer feel and have better long-term launderability than acrylics.

If you are painting a fabric piece in which softness is not an issue (a canvas floor mat or a tote bag, for instance), acrylics provide good durability. When using inks for printing and stamping, a "vehicle" is often required. This clear, thick substance allows you to keep the ink pigments workable and of even consistency as you roll or dab the ink onto the stamp or printing block. There are many oil-based inks on the market, and recently a water-based product has become available at many art supply stores. Paints

for stenciling come in cake form. Stenciling can also be done with spray paint.

When working with paints in metal cans, cleanup is important. Unless you remove all of the paint from the rim of the can, the lid will not seal, and your paint may be ruined. Cover the tip of a screwdriver or paint stick with a rag and run the rag around the rim of the can, to remove all the paint from the groove where the lid sits. When the groove is clean, tap the lid on with a hammer or the handle of the screwdriver. Proper sealing will preserve expensive paints and prevent having to throw chemical waste into our landfills. Proper sealing will enable you to use up the entire can of paint.

Notes on Brushes

Brushes are identified by the size and shape of the ferrule (the metal tube that attaches the bristles to the handle), round or flat; by the type of bristles (natural or synthetic, soft or coarse); and by the shape that the bristles form. Natural bristles (sable and squirrel, for example) are wonderful to use and easy to

reshape. However, they are expensive, and when using acrylics, glues, and other synthetic paints, they are not necessary. The higher-quality, newer synthetic brushes offer as much control as a natural brush.

Many of the problems encountered in decorative painting stem from using distorted, stiff brushes. Part of the trick of brush control is in well-trained bristles that can be counted on to bend properly as you move the brush. Mistreated brushes often have stray bristles that pop out and spray paint onto your project at the worst times! Always clean your brushes thoroughly with soap and warm water, and if they have soft bristles, reshape them gently to their original form. Store dry brushes flat, or with the bristles upward, so that they are not being distorted by other brushes in the container. Wet brushes should be reshaped and carefully rolled in paper towel or newspaper.

Artist's brushes are numbered from low (smallest) to high (largest) with either a corresponding diameter (for round) or width (for flat) noted. Brushes with extra-long bristles, called liner brushes, are excellent for painting thin outlines. Oval brushes are flat with an oval silhouette, and are great for decorative painting, since you can turn the brush one way for thick lines; twist to get a medium, rounded shape; and turn the other way for a thin, flat line. Stencil brushes are round, and have coarse bristles for pushing paint directly downward into the stencil shape without extending beyond the stencil mask.

When you paint, "fill" the brush with paint; that is, get lots of paint into the upper part of the brush and then wipe the lower half of the bristles onto the lip of your jar or palette. As you put pressure on the brush, paint will flow out of the tips of the bristles.

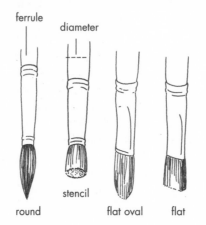

ferrule

diameter

round

stencil

flat oval

flat

Plan your moves. The trick to painting graceful stems is in knowing where you're going to start and end, and which parts you want thick and thin. Starting at the thick end, with the brush under some pressure, and pulling away as you ease up on the brush pressure, will give you a line that gets gradually thinner until you come to the end and can carefully pull up and use the brush shape to create a clean finish to your stroke.

Practice is really the best way to learn to control a brush.

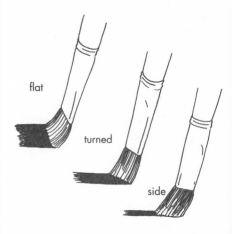

flat

turned

side

STENCILING

Stenciling is the process of applying paint within a predesigned cutout (stencil). It can be applied to any surface but works best on flat areas. You can buy stencils at craft stores. These are usually made by machine, out of thin plastic or Mylar. Since a stencil is a negative of the image you will be creating, it masks the background of the shape and you fill the empty spaces with color. Stencils are also easy to make. You can cut them out of Mylar or acetate — available at art supply stores — or stencil paper, which is a thin, flexible, wax-coated cardboard. If you use the stencil paper, you will have to trace the design directly onto the paper (using carbon paper) before you cut it, or use a light box to view your image through the paper. Acetate and Mylar are clear, so you can see through them to cut them out. You will need a very sharp X-acto-type knife, preferably with a swivel blade if your design has many curves. The design must be made in such a way that the shapes are divided by ⅛"–¼" borders, which will become the background of the finished pattern.

Stencils are filled in using stencil paint, a semisolid cream that is dabbed into the stencil brush. The stencil brush has coarse bristles with a flat end.

A two-part stencil, with registration marks indicated at the corners.

The brush is then dabbed or rubbed into the open areas of the stencil, being kept perpendicular to the paper to avoid pushing paint under the stencil edges. Spray mount, a product that allows you temporarily to adhere the stencil to the surface, can be used to hold the stencil down and eliminate the possibility of pushing paint underneath the edges. Colors can be blended directly on the painting surface. Creme paints must cure for 48 hours before you can use the painted product.

Stencils can also be spray painted with standard cans of spray paint, with spray bottles of premixed color, or with an airbrush and airbrush inks. Hold the sprayer perpendicular to the surface you are decorating, or the paint will shoot underneath the stencil edges.

Many stencils can be used to create repeat patterns. Measure along a wall or across a surface the distance desired between repeats of the pattern and then lay the stencil down at the preestablished marks. You can make registration holes in the corners of your stencil; they will help you locate the proper layout. These would not be painted through (mask them with tape if you are spraying), but you can see through them to locate the marks you have made on the painting surface. If your design is 3″ x 6″ and you want it to repeat after a 4″ space, mark the 3″ x 6″ pattern with chalk, locate a mark 4″ away on all sides, and mark the 3″ x 6″ pattern again. The chalk can be rubbed off after the paint has dried.

STAMPING

Stamping uses oil- or water-based paints or inks. You can use store-bought rubber stamps; Indian batik stamps made of wood; or make your own stamps of sponge, potato, or rubber.

Cut sponges into simple shapes using scissors. Potatoes — the larger and older the better — are cut with a knife or a cookie cutter. Trace the shape onto the cut surface of the potato; then slice into the potato meat about ½" all around your design. Trim away the excess potato. Let the potato rest, cut side down, on paper towels for a few minutes, to drain out as much potato juice as possible. It is important to cut the surface of the potato as straight as possible in order to have a flat printing surface.

If you are ambitious and good with a knife, you can make

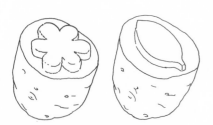

Potato stamps are easy to make and effective.

a rubber stamp from a large rubber eraser. It can be hard to cut, but many art stores carry soft eraser rubber. If you can cut them carefully, these stamps will last much longer than potatoes or sponges.

Applying the Paint or Ink

There are three ways to ink your stamps.

1 Direct: Put paint onto a flat surface such as a plastic plate. Dip the stamp into the paint. The drawback to this method, although it works best for sponges, is that you have very little control over how much paint goes onto the stamp, and may have to do a test print or wipe paint off to prevent a smudgy, blotty print.

2 Paint Pad: This is a homemade version of a stamp pad (the kind that comes with an uninked rubber stamp). You will need a shallow plastic container, a sponge, and a piece of cotton muslin or sheeting. Cut the sponge to fit inside the plastic container. Cover the sponge with the fabric and fit it into the plastic container. Stir your paint; thin it if necessary. Pour

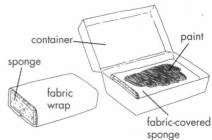

A homemade stamp pad

the paint onto the paint pad and push on the fabric/sponge with the back of a spoon to bring some paint back up to the surface. Press the stamp onto the pad, and it is inked!

3 Roller: Rollers (also called brayers), commonly used in linoleum block printing, are available in art stores and craft shops. You will need a flat, surface, like glass or plexiglass, and paint that is not too runny. Pour some paint onto the surface and roll it back and forth until the roller is covered but not dripping. Now roll paint onto the surface of your stamp.

You may stamp on any surface; the surface and end use will determine the type of paint you'll want. Stamping can be random, or you can repeat patterns onto surfaces that you

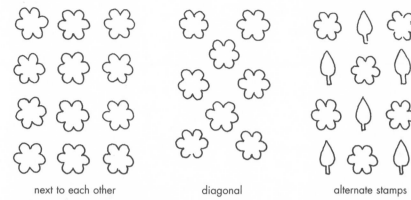

next to each other   diagonal   alternate stamps

Some simple stamping patterns

have premarked at set intervals. Depending on the product you are making and the size of the stamp, you can repeat the pattern right next to the previous image, or leave a space in between, or alternate diagonally, like bricklaying.

You might make three different stamps and alternate them, so you would need to mark out the distance you need to leave between them.

NATURE PRINTING

This technique is similar to stamping, but you will be using various plant materials as stamps, thus transferring their shapes, veins, and textures onto the decorative surface. The information presented here was adapted from *Nature Printing* (see page 124).

Choose relatively flat, heavily veined or textured leaves to start with. If you are collecting out in the field, use a spray bottle to keep the leaves moist and carefully place them in a zip-seal bag with air blown into it. Press the items, using a flower press or a thick telephone book, soon after collecting them. Always press between layers of absorbent, unprinted paper (paper towel or newsprint). For printing, you don't have to press the specimens until they dry. In fact, they should remain somewhat moist and supple, so if they do dry, respray them, put them in a plastic bag in the refrigerator overnight, and press them again in absorbent paper for 30 minutes or longer, just enough to flatten them.

If you want to print with bulkier items, try to press them somewhat flat, arranging the petals or leaves in a pleasant pattern as you lay them out, being aware that the shapes toward the surface will be the shapes that receive the ink.

Block-printing ink is the easiest product to use. If you use oil-based inks, you will need linseed or poppyseed oil as a wetting vehicle. Inks are also available in a water-based version with a vehicle to keep them wet. For fabric, you can use textile paints with extender, or, if you don't wash the fabric for at least 4 weeks, the block-printing inks will set colorfast onto the fabric. For paper, it is possible to use tube watercolor paints; these must be painted onto the plant rather than rolled on, but can result in some beautiful color blending. Acrylics, oils, and etching and lithography inks also work for this technique. Be sure to use acrylic medium to keep the acrylic paints wet longer.

Applying the Ink to the Plant Material

Stamp pad: Use a purchased stamp pad, or the paint pad described in the Stamping section of this chapter.

Brayers: Soft rubber rollers are used to set ink directly onto the plant material.

Brushes: A relatively stiff brush is best to apply paint to plant material. Brushes are used predominantly for applying watercolor to plant material for printing on paper only.

Dabbers: Dabbers are a piece of foam on a stick, easily made with a bottle cork or dowel and a circle of vinyl foam (¼" thick) or a cosmetic sponge attached to it with a rubber band.

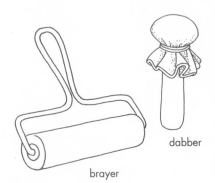

dabber

brayer

Variations and Hints ∽

∽ Use two palettes — one for rolling out the ink and the other for inking the leaves.

∽ Instead of inking in just one color, ink the palette with two or three colors in the smear and roll on a rainbow of hues.

∽ Use a brush to highlight veins directly on the leaf before printing it.

∽ For three-dimensional flowers, pods, and fruit, add ink or paint to the surfaces of the plant material you wish to print. Use the plant material as you would a stamp, pushing it into the paper as carefully as possible. This can be done with vegetables (the open inside of a green bean), fruit (half an apple, with the core and seeds exposed), or flowers.

∽ Dabbers can be used to push ink into overlapping petals without crushing them, as a roller would. They can also be used to add dabs of color to an already inked piece.

∽ If you are printing a large item and want to print several leaves at once, make a simple walking press. You will need a 2' x 3' sheet of plywood and a piece of heavy wool felt (or layers of newspaper) twice that size. Lay the felt on the wood, leaving half of it to double over the printing. Put a piece of newsprint on the felt. Put your printing paper or fabric on the newsprint. Place the leaves and other inked plant materials on the printing surface, ink side down. Be sure that you have added plenty of extender, oil, or vehicle, so that the inks stay wet while you compose your print. When your composition is complete, lay another sheet of newsprint over the leaves, then the felt blanket. Carefully walk over the entire surface, taking small steps, so that you press each and every inked item onto the printing surface, without moving them around on the page.

BASIC METHOD

1 Roll out the ink, thinned with oil or vehicle, or paints onto a palette of glass, plexiglass, or waxed paper. Keep a palette knife or strip of cardboard handy to move ink around, since you will need to keep a consistent smear of ink under the roller.

2 Place a pressed leaf, underside up, onto a clean part of the palette and roll over it with the inked brayer, or dab ink onto it with a dabber.

3 Carefully pick up the leaf with tweezers and place it onto the printing surface, ink side down. Lay another sheet of paper or paper towel over it and press with the heel of your hand, the back of a spoon, a clean brayer, or a rolling pin, taking care not to move the leaf once it touches the paper.

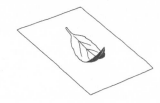

4 Carefully pull up the paper and remove the leaf with the tweezers.

WRAPPING IDEAS

Stamping is a great craft to do with children. Making wrapping paper on newsprint is fun, easy, and appreciated by the kids and the gift recipients. Follow the instructions for stamping with sponges and potatoes, or, for an even messier version, stamp thinned down white glue, and sprinkle glitter on it — the result will be glittered shapes that kids really love. (The grown-up version of this is to use embossing powder or gold leaf.)

Kitchen gifts wrapped in towels can be a great project. Buy plain white flour sack towels, or buy fabric yardage and hem or fringe the edges. Use any of the stencil, stamp, or printing techniques to make a fabric wrapper that echoes the herbs used in the culinary gift you are offering. I like to include recipes that help the recipient get started using the vinegar or herb gift.

Gift cards decorated at the same time as the wrapping can be made to perfectly match the paper or fabric. I keep old manila file folders around, and cut cards out of the clean parts. While you have the paint and

inks out, and are working with the sponges, potatoes, and leaves, print some matching cards.

You can also make printed ribbon, by cutting strips of cotton fabric, and printing leaves down their length. Even a plain paper package looks great with a hand printed ribbon.

Make tiny bouquets from garden flowers or herbs, and tie them to the outside of the package.

Around the holidays, and particularly for my friends who like to do beadwork (and need to wax their thread), I melt beeswax in the top of a double boiler, and pour it into ornament molds, available from candle and soap suppliers. A short length of gold cord in the hot wax acts as a hanger, and when the holiday is over, they can save it for next year, or wax their beading thread with it all year.

Baskets filled with theme gifts are always appreciated. I find baskets at yard sales, and use them for food, cosmetic, and gardening gifts — they make a nice way to give a gift in a reusable container, and who doesn't like baskets?

Make a custom box, following the basic format outlined in the Decoupaged Seed File Box project on pages 72–73. Cover it with self-adhesive contact paper. It will be sturdy enough to become a storage box for "things" (we all collect "things," don't we?). Purchase the contact paper in several colors and/or patterns, and make a patchwork box decorated with your own shapes.

I save every interesting tidbit I can. I have broken earrings, plastic flowers, pieces of kids' toys, curtain rings, feathers, and rubber gaskets, to name a few. I keep them all in a box, and when I'm feeling creative, but uninspired, I rummage through my box of "junk," and find "free stuff" to play with. Almost anything can become something else, with a little glue, ribbon, and imagination.

SOURCE LIST

MISCELLANEOUS ARTS AND CRAFTS SUPPLIES

Craftime, Inc.
P.O. Box 93706
Atlanta, GA 30377
(800) 849-8463

Craft King
P.O. Box 90637
Lakeland, FL 33804
888-CRAFTY-1

Dharma Trading Company
P.O. Box 150916
San Rafael, CA 94915
(800) 542-5227

Dick Blick
P.O. Box 1267
Galesburg, IL 61402
(800) 447-8192

Sax Arts and Crafts
P.O. Box 510710
New Berlin, WI 53151
(800) 558-6696

HERBS, SPICES, OILS

Atlantic Spice Co.
P.O. Box 205
North Truro, MA 02652
(508) 487-6100

The Essential Oil Company
P.O. Box 206
Lake Oswego, OR 97034
(800) 729-5912

Lavender Lane
P.O. Box 7265
Citrus Heights, CA 95621
(916) 334-4400

Lebermuth Co., Inc.
P.O. Box 4103
South Bend, IN 46634
(800) 648-1123

Lorann Oils
P.O. Box 22009
Lansing, MI 48909
(800) 248-1302

Penn Herb Co., Ltd.
10601 Decatur Rd. Ste. #2
Philadelphia, PA 19154
(800) 523-9971

The Rosemary House
120 S. Market Street
Mechanicsburg, PA 17055
(717) 697-5111

San Francisco Herb and Natural
    Food Co.
4744 Kato Road
Fremont, CA 94538
(800) 227-2830

CANDLEMAKING SUPPLIES AND WAX

Barker Enterprises
15106 10th Avenue SW
Seattle, WA 98166
(800) 543-0601

Pourette Mfg. Co.
P.O. Box 19056
Seattle, WA 98115
(800) 888-WICK

Walnut Hill Enterprises
Green Lane and Wilson Avenue
Bristol, PA 19007
(215) 785-6511

Yaley Enterprises, Inc.
7672 Avianca Drive
Redding, CA 96002
(916) 365-5252

POLYMER CLAY

American Art Clay Co., Inc.
4717 W 16th St.
Indianapolis, IN 46222
(800) 374-1600

Clay Factory of Escondido
P.O. Box 460598
Escondido, CA 92046
(619) 741-3242

CLOCK MOVEMENTS

Cherry Hill Toys, Inc.
P.O. Box 369
Belmont, OH 43718
(614) 484-4363

Klockit
P.O. Box 636
Lake Geneva, WI 53147
(800) 566-2548

Precision Movements
4283 Chestnut St.
P.O. Box 689
Emmaus, PA 18049
(800) 533-2024

GLASSWARE AND SCIENTIFIC SUPPLIES

American Science and Surplus
3605 Howard Street
Skokie, IL 60076
(847) 982-0870

Chemlab
1060 Ortega Way Unit C
Placentia, CA 92670
(714) 630-7902

COTTON FABRICS

Mission Valley Textiles
P.O. Box 311357
New Braunfels, TX 78131
(800) 628-2513

Testfabrics, Inc.
P.O. Box 420
Middlesex, NJ 08846
(908) 469-6446

INDEX

Page references in italic indicate illustrations

OTHER STOREY TITLES YOU WILL ENJOY

At Home with Herbs: Inspiring Ideas for Cooking, Crafts, Decorating, and Cosmetics, by Jane Newdick. More than 100 inspiring yet practical herbal craft projects. 224 pages. Hardcover. ISBN 0-88266-886-2.

The Essential Oils Book: Creating Personal Blends for Mind and Body, by Colleen K. Dodt. A rich resource on the many uses of aromatherapy. Simple recipes use ingredients available locally. 160 pages. Paperback. ISBN 0-88266-913-3.

Candlemaker's Companion, by Betty Oppenheimer. Step-by-step instructions, history, vocabulary, and basic math of candlemaking. Includes information on materials and equipment. 176 pages. Paperback. ISBN 0-88266-994-X.

Gifts for Bird Lovers: Over 50 Projects to Make and Give, by Althea Sexton. Step-by-step instructions and illustrations for creating over forty projects. 128 pages. Paperback. ISBN 0-88266-981-8.

The Herbal Body Book: A Natural Approach to Healthier Hair, Skin, and Nails, by Stephanie Tourles. More than 100 recipes for facial scrubs, hair rinses, shampoos, soaps, cleansing lotions, moisturizers, lip balms, toothpaste, powders, insect repellents, and more. 128 pages. Paperback. ISBN 0-88266-880-3.

Herbal Treasures: Inspiring Month-by-Month Projects for Gardening, Cooking, and Crafts, by Phyllis V. Shaudys. A compendium of the best herb crafts, recipes, and gardening ideas. 320 pages. Paperback. ISBN 0-88266-618-5.

Herbal Vinegar, by Maggie Oster. Ideas for making and flavoring inexpensive herb, spice, vegetable, and flower vinegars. More than 100 recipes for using flavored vinegars in everything from appetizers to entrees. Vinegar-based personal and household uses and hints. 176 pages. Paperback. ISBN 0-88266-843-9. Hardcover. ISBN 0-88266-876-5.

The Herb Gardener: A Guide for All Seasons, by Susan McClure. Complete instructions on every conceivable aspect of herbs in the home and garden. 240 pages. Paperback. ISBN 0-88266-873-0.

Herb Mixtures & Spicy Blends, edited by Deborah Balmuth. An essential guide to dozens of easy-to-make mixtures. 160 pages. Paperback. ISBN 0-88266-918-4. Hardcover. ISBN 0-88266-919-2.

Herbs for Weddings & Other Celebrations: A Treasury of Recipes, Gifts & Decorations, by Bertha Reppert. Step-by-step instructions for seventy-five projects, from wreaths and baskets to invitations and buffet dishes. 200 pages. Paperback. ISBN 0-88266-864-1. Hardcover. ISBN 0-88266-866-8.

Making Your Own Paper,: by Marianne Saddington. Instructions on using a mold, pressing and drying, coloring and texturing. 96 pages. Paperback. ISBN 0-88266-784-X.

Natural BabyCare: Pure and Soothing Recipes and Techniques for Mothers and Babies, by Colleen K. Dodt. Easy-to-follow instructions for natural lotions, bath and massage oils, creams, powders, and shampoos. Special features on self-care during pregnancy and childbirth, infant massage techniques, and gift ideas. 144 pages. Paperback. ISBN 0-88266-953-2.

The Natural Soap Book: Making Herbal and Vegetable-Based Soaps, by Susan Miller Cavitch. How to make soap without chemical additives and synthetic ingredients. Along with basic vegetable-based soap recipes, ideas on scenting, coloring, cutting, trimming, and wrapping soaps. 144 pages. Paperback. ISBN 0-88266-888-9.

Nature Printing with Herbs, Fruits, and Flowers, by Laura Donnelly Bethmann. Step-by-step instructions for collecting specimens, designing artwork, and printing, accompanied by color photos and illustrations. 96 pages. Hardcover. ISBN 0-88266-929-X.

These books and other Storey books are available at your bookstore, farm store, garden center, or directly from Storey Publishing, Schoolhouse Road, Pownal, Vermont 05261, or by calling 1-800-441-5700. www.storey.com